D1242558

ON DISPLAY vol. 2

Sturmgeschütz III

Foreword

The Sturmgeschütz Assault Gun was a German self-propelled weapon at the disposal of infantry divisions – so they could rely on quick and easy artillery support of their own. Artillery fire support systems are generally not that complicated and were established during several wars but with the same reasoning… troops need back-up.

Near the soldiers in question, an observation post would be installed to have a direct view over possible target grounds, along with communications with the troop to be supported - and with the gun position somewhere behind. The distance to the firing position depends on the firing range of the guns being used. In most cases, the gun crews are not as close to the target area so they can see it themselves.

When fire support is requested by the troops, the observation posts measure and report the target's location to the firing position. There the azimuth, elevation and necessary ammunition requirements are calculated, then communicated to the guns for eventual firing. Continuous corrections are given by the observer to the gun positions, for fixing enemy movements or to cope with weather/environmental changes.

That indirect firing of classic artillery, just described, is quite slow in bringing fire to the target, due the necessary work chain. Matters worsen and even become more complex, when the supported troops have to move; the artillery installations must, sooner or later, move too and this temporarily halts the ability to fire.

While moving the guns, whether they are vehicle- or horse-drawn, reconnaissance units must geographically measure new firing positions and prepare them for the guns, giving data to the fire control centre for its calculations. Also, while guns are being moved, the observer teams have to search for new positions and install themselves and, install new radio and/or cable communications. When the guns arrive, they have to be unlimbered and properly positioned in their new firing positions. Then, the slow artillery is again ready to let steel rain from the sky.

Another disadvantage of classic artillery was, particularly in World War Two, that there was never enough of it! So many troops did not get artillery support at all; usually the division commander decided which of his troops would be supported, depending on the situation. All of those factors hindered the support of fast-moving infantry troops, not to speak of motorised or even armoured armies. Fire was often provided too late to give instant, direct support to mobile troops.

The German Army gave infantry guns of 7.5cm and 15cm calibre to the infantry divisions, to put short-distance fire support in their own hands, mostly for direct firing. This gave infantry commanders a certain independence concerning fire back-up, but the guns were heavy and slow too move – still not sufficient for faster and mobile warfare a world away from the trenches of World War One. Along came General von Manstein's suggestion in the 1930s, to place an artillery

On Display vol.2 - StuG III

© Canfora Grafisk Form & Förlag 2012
ISBN 978-91-976773-7-0
Project manager: Toni Canfora
Design: Mike Rinaldi, Toni Canfora
Print: Uniprint, Tallin, Estonia

Canfora Grafisk Form & Förlag
Upplandsgatan 61
113 28 Stockholm
Sweden
info@canfora.se - www.canfora.se

gun on a fully-tracked chassis. The German army and industry did exactly that, using a Panzerkampfwagen III chassis in combination with modified 7.5cm tank gun for trials; eventually, a formidable weapon was developed. The gun was placed on a stand as deep into the chassis as possible (to ensure a low profile for the vehicle), housed below an armoured superstructure, or casemate. Tests were successful and an order to build that new weapon, branded 'Sturmgeschütz', was awarded to the Daimler-Benz factory in Berlin. Voluntary troops were trained in new Sturmartillerie units. Although production should have started in autumn 1939, it took some months to begin series manufacture, although the first batteries were equipped for the campaign against France in May 1940.

So, the baptism of fire for the Sturmgeschütze was in the France and, it performed its task very well. During 1940/41, time was used to create several more Sturmartillerie units, to be ready for Operation Barbarossa. Manufacturing was displaced to Alkett, in Berlin. During the war against Russia, the Sturmgeschütze became used as a mobile anti-tank defence. In fact, there was more ammunition fired at enemy tanks than against real infantry targets, such as pillboxes, machine gun nests, anti-tank guns, etc

In spring 1942 this fact was accepted and the Sturmgeschütz was given a longer gun, which was able to destroy tanks at a longer distance. Its new role as a tank hunter, besides that of direct fire support, was established. Better radio equipment and a larger superstructure were introduced and, on the eve of 1942, the Sturmgeschütz gained its final form...the so called Ausfüh-

rung (Variant) G. In February 1943, MIAG joined Alkett as a second manufacturer to boost the output of Sturmgeschütze even further. During 1943, thickening of the frontal armour, from 50mm to 80mm was undertaken to ensure protection as enemy tanks became more powerful.

From May 1943, Sturmgeschütze were deployed not only with the Sturmartillerie itself, but as a stop-gap in tank battalions, too. In June, 1944, official records claim 20,000 enemy tanks destroyed by Sturmgeschütze.

By the close of the war, some 9,200 Sturmgeschütze had been produced, along with 1,200 Sturmhaubitzen (assault howitzer). If one wishes to model a tank that is typically German, then in most cases the Tiger or Panther is the first thought...but the Sturmgeschütze were unique! So, modelling these pieces of war technology is something quintessentially German and something other nations did not have; the tank hunter concept was, however, widely copied.

This book presents examples beautifully modelled Sturmgeschütze, built to properly emulate the real thing. Packing the guns into a historic scene promotes even more realism and life to the mighty assault gun. For modellers keen on Sturmgeschütze, this book gives much sage advice for building them well and accurately. Indeed, for all modellers it offers inspiration for harmonious, life-like dioramas. I'm sure you'll be as excited about it as I am!

August, 2012
Peter Müller, History Facts

Introduction

Most modellers experience days when things don't go as planned and when the results are not as we'd hoped. In most cases, though, we raise our heads high and come back with renewed vigour. Essentially, most models can be saved if something has gone wrong and it usually just comes down to how stubborn you are, as long as the feeling for the model is not lost.

Things go wrong in publishing too, but that usually happens long before the finished product reaches the hands of the customer and, fortunately, before the presses start to roll. Some of you may recall that OnDisplay Vol. 2 was announced several years ago, and was actually supposed to be a diorama book - but then a very unpredictable thing happened. Thieves broke into my former office and my computer and back-up disk were stolen. Along with them, several of the articles for the book disappeared and hundreds of step-by-step photos were lost, beyond re-creation in the short term.

Afterwards I started to assess the damage. Could this book still be produced? I quickly came to the conclusion that it would take at least 6-10 months to re-gain what had been lost. Worse still, I had lost the inspiration so vital when producing a book, and simply put it on hold – as many of us do with certain modelling projects.

So, instead of a diorama book we now have a title on the StuG III, something that had been on my mind for several years. To me, the StuG symbolises the backbone of the German fighting forces; always in the thick of the action and on nearly every front. German infantrymen must have felt a certain degree of comfort knowing that StuGs lay in support, without having to wait for them to be assigned through a bureaucratic chain of command. After proper study, one will find that StuGs seem to be everywhere in wartime photos, reminding us of their importance on the battlefield.

The focus of this book is not to impart a history lesson on the StuG, as others do that far better and with greater depth. Still, as you will find, great attention has been paid to re-creating the StuGs here as accurately as possible. Many hours have gone into researching them. What I hope in the end is that the builds will prove to be a valuable source of inspiration, and a guide to help achieve the results you want with your model. I also hope that the great variety of versions, camouflage schemes and theatres of operation will appeal to the majority. The StuG is one of the few vehicles that served in great numbers throughout the war, therefore providing modellers with seemingly endless opportunities.

During this book's production, I have found myself to be highly privileged by working with great people and talented modellers. Their skills and ideas constantly amaze and inspire, the effect being that I now want to build every possible version of the StuG. Without them, this book would never have seen the light of day. Finally, I would also like to extend my gratitude to Peter Müller from History Facts, for all his support in this project. Thank you all.

Toni Canfora

Contents

StuG III Ausf. A, Sturmgeschütz Batterie 640
InfantrieRegiment „Großdeutschland"

On the cut of the sickle

The reckless advance to the west
Near Amiens, France, 20th May 1940

ON THE CUT OF THE SICKLE

Text and model by
Volker Bembennek

German modeller Volker Bembennek builds an impressive diorama full of story and skill.
This time he focuses his efforts on the earliest of the StuG III family, the Ausf. A.

In 1937, five prototypes of the so-called 0-series based on the PzKpfw III Ausf B were produced and were extensively tested in the following months…and in January 1940 the mass production of the Version A began.

The production order of 30 vehicles was awarded to Daimler-Benz, but this would remain the only version of the StuG III produced by this company. All other versions were manufactured by Alkett and Miag.

Based on the chassis of the PzKpfw III Ausf F (5 ZW), the A version also displayed the same properties. The hull was adapted to the interpretation of the StuG III and the frontal armour was increased from 30mm to 50mm. The two emergency hatches on each side of the hull were removed. Specific characteristics which mark out the A version from its contemporaries, include:

- 38cm tracks (Typ Kgs 6111/380/120)
- Narrow road wheels (520x75 - 397)
- Narrow sprocket wheel with eight circular recesses
- Disk-shaped idler wheel with oval cutouts for weight reduction
- The distance of the three return rollers on each side was equally large
- Un-armoured smoke grenade launchers on the rear of the vehicle
- The bullet deflector before the gunner's sight was built from individually welded rectangular profiles
- A one-piece 10m tow rope on the engine cover
- A storage box on the left and the right of the rear part of the fenders
- No Notek night march unit, but two round, split tail and brake lights
- Arrangement of the roof flaps above the gunner; the front hatch with one hinge and the rear hatch with two hinges
- No antenna channel, but an additional hook beside the left storage box

The assault artillery batteries 640, 659, 660 and 665 were equipped with the 30 vehicles built by Daimler-Benz. These vehicles were used for the first time in France, and by all accounts worked outstandingly.

Sturmgeschütz-battery 640

On November 1, 1939, Assault Gun Battery 640 made its debut as the first combat unit of the 'storm artillery' in Jüter-bog. From mid-April 1940, the unit was assigned to the infantry regiment Groß-deutschland and was equipped with six guns in each of the three platoons.

During the French campaign, starting from May 10, 1940, the vehicles were involved in the fighting in Bastogne, at Sedan and at Stonne, at Dunkirk and at Amiens; likewise, on the advance to Lyon.

During the campaign, the vehicles were already modified by the troops during the initial weeks, and adapted to their appropriate needs and requirements. Thus, one recognizes on different original photographs that especially the narrow road wheels had been replaced very early on by the broader versions. These had, due to the broader rubber linings, greater stability and were more hard-wearing than the narrower variants. Accordingly, we often see a mix of narrow and wide wheels on the chassis, and several spare wheels were usually carried. Also, spare track links were hung (for lack of suitable mounting plates) at the towing eyes either at the vehicle's nose or at the rear, and were carried in large quantities.

Another frequently observed modification was the attachment of an improvised railing at the rear engine deck, in order to create more stowage space for various pieces of equipment.

As a paragon for my model of a Sturmgeschütz III A version, I have chosen this

unit and the appropriate time period. On the basis of various original recordings, but also with the liberty of my own interpretation, I have tried to arrange the model as interestingly as possible.

Preparation

The DML kit of the Ausf. A is already rather old, but nevertheless makes a good overall impression. Besides its reasonably accurate dimensions, the replication of typical Ausf. A features is fairly satisfactory. At least as a starting point for further detailing, this kit can be described as being a good foundation. Nevertheless, I at least partly resorted to the chassis components of the Tamiya's Sturmgeschütz III G (Early), which exhibits a considerable degree of better detail. Of course, the new Tamiya kit of the StuG III Ausf.B (35281) would provide for the conversion, but there are several kits of the early G variant in my stash, which I often refer to for such refinements and modifications. But before the real work begins on the model, you should first go through a thoughtful planning phase and consider the final presentation of the model you want to create. These relate both to the details which should be revised, the modifications which were made by the troops and also likely damages. Likewise, one should study the instructions of the upgrade sets to familiarize one's self with its contents.

The lower hull and suspension

On the lower hull I decided to use most of the parts from the Tamiya kit, since these showed more accurate dimensions and sharper detail, when compared to certain scale drawings. The lower hull from the Dragon kit can be used, and I would not describe it as bad, just lacking the degree of detail. Also, parts from the Dragon kit are needed for the completion of this section.

The first larger modification coincided with the first work procedure, since the front return roller on both sides of the lo-

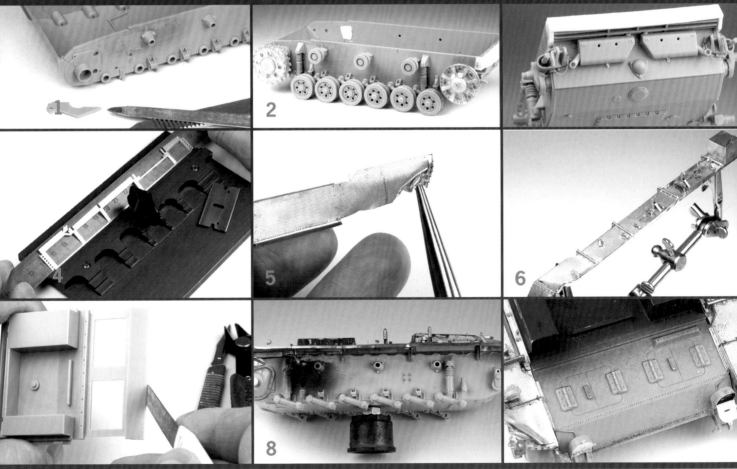

1-3 The front return roller mounts were cut out with a mini-disc saw and a sharp scalpel. The hole was sealed with a piece of plastic sheet, then filled and sanded with Tamiya Putty. Moulded-on towing eyes on Tamiya parts B6 and B7 were removed, since these did not exist on the Ausf. A. Also, parts B8 & B9, the track tensioning devices, must be modified; the clamping screw with spindle had to be shifted to the rear. The narrow Dragon road wheels had to be drilled out so they fitted on the suspension arms. Also, the Friul idler wheels were modified with a piece of plastic hub (Tamiya kit) to ensure a tight fit. The air outlet of the engine had to be re-built completely from plastic sheet. Also, note the early version of the maintenance fan belt cover from the Dragon hull. 4 Large PE parts were formed with a dedicated bending tool. 5 Damage was caused with the help of flat-nosed pliers. 6 The finished soldered left fender, ready for installation. 7 The brackets for the kit fenders were removed cleanly. 8 The left side showing the modifica-

ON THE CUT OF THE SICKLE

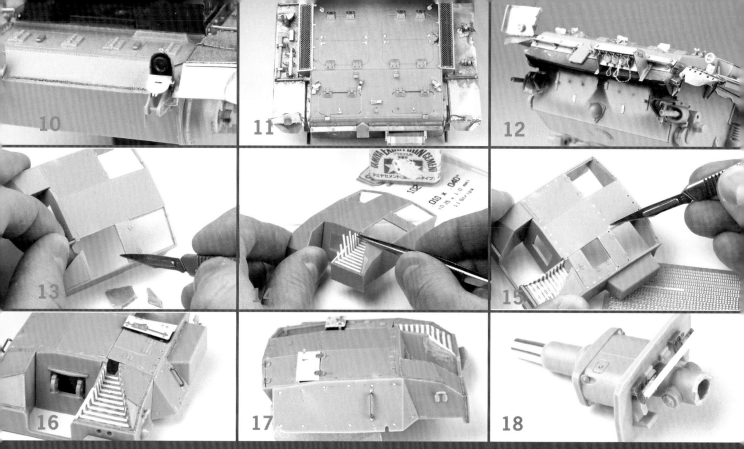

tions to the return roller and fenders; the four bolts present on the driver's seat are from Bronco, while the early 'shocks' are from the Dragon kit. **9-10** The gear cover with the revised projectile deflector before the driver's view and, the newly applied hatch closures from Lion Roar. **11** All hinges on the engine deck were slightly drilled out. Furthermore, all brackets for the tow rope and the closures of the hatches were removed. **12** Connection angles between upper and lower hull were supplemented by etched parts from Lion Roar and, refined with screw heads from Calibre35. The smoke grenade launcher was constructed entirely with photo-etched parts. **13** The area above the gunner had to be cut out cleanly to subsequently be replaced by component M9 from Dragon. **14** I rebuilt the new viewing channel with thin Evergreen plastic strips (0.25mm x 1.5mm). **15** The superstructure pins were removed, before the careful rendering of small holes. The holes were re-drilled and screw heads added from Aber set 35A101. **16-17** Additional superstructure armor was added in the same way and, handles were replaced with copper wire. **18** Plastic material and parts from the Aber set were used for the representation of detail behind the gun shield.

wer hull had to be shifted some millimetres to the rear. For this I carefully cut out the entire cast-on mounting of the return rollers and blocked the resulting holes with a suitable piece of plastic sheet. After some putty and a subsequent sanding of the areas, the previously separated and cleaned mountings can be attached at the new positions. For this, one should defer again to accurate scale drawings (distance of the return rollers on the model in each case being 30mm).

Next I continued with detailing work on the front of the vehicle, by attaching Tamiya's parts B6 and B7. Prior to this, however, the cast-on eyes of the towing device must be cleanly removed since these did not exist on the early versions.

The wheel suspensions, suspension arms and the stop blocks can be assembled according to the Tamiya instructions. But the four shock absorbers, however, are the early versions from the Dragon kit (parts G4 and G5). Also the Tamiya components B8 and B9, which represent track tensioning devices, have to be altered accordingly prior to installation; the tightening screw with spindle must be shifted to the rear and later protrudes rearwards over the idler wheels. For representation of the track I decided to use the extremely realistic single link track from Friul Model, and therefore I also choose the sprocket wheels and the idler wheels from this company. The components were all of excellent quality and had to be modified

only slightly. With the road wheels I decided to follow what was seen in reference photographs, and mixed the narrow version from the Dragon kit with the broader units from Tamiya's boxing. As a final step in the construction of the lower hull, focus turned to the rear area. The Tamiya part B3 can be installed here without any change. The maintenance cover for the fan belt, however, was carefully separated from Dragon part A3, since this is the early version with only three screws. The exhaust and towing devices were used unchanged from the Tamiya kit. A closing, but larger modification was the representation of the engine air outlet. Tamiya's component B19 cannot be used here, since this represents the later version

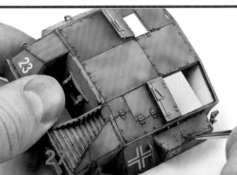

19-20 The finished model without paint. Figures for the final scene were dry-fitted for testing purposes, as were most of the details, since the model had to be again completely disassembled for painting. **21** The camouflage pattern was drawn on side view copies. This was done with the help of several original photographs and drawings. **22** After pre-shading all edges and recesses with a black-brown color, all large surfaces were coated with primer red. **23-24** After this, I mixed the grey base colour; dark grey, which was lightened gradually. To create a more pleasing tone, I mixed a colour that leaned towards blue. The whole thing thereby seems more alive and visually pleasing. Individual areas were masked with the help of trimmed paper templates, in order to imitate the direction of the light toward the vehicle. By this measure, the various surfaces, edges and angles

of the vehicle can be better emphasised and the entire model gets more depth. 25-26 The camouflage pattern, in which the brown approximately covers one-third of the vehicle's surface. The shapes of these patches should preferably extend longitudinally over corners and edges to visually break up these areas. Here again, lighter and darker areas were processed according to the incidence of light. The vehicle markings, consisting of Balkenkreuz and videntification numbers, as well as the tactical sign on the left front fender, were represented with dry transfers from Archer. 27-29 Careful painting of the chipping on the casemate; here one should proceed in a logical manner and especially work on areas that are entered by the crew, or infantry. Otherwise, it is always advisable to start at the edges and corners of the armour plates with the paint damage and to spare large areas as much as possible. After two or three passes the paint damage is finished. A good recommendation is to not entirely apply the paint chipping in one day, but to distribute it over several applications. .

starting from version F/8. Unfortunately, one cannot rely on the Dragon kit, as this segment is moulded on the lower hull. So, I built this component from scratch with the help of plastic sheet. A big help here, again, were several scale drawings.

The upper hull

On the upper hull, with exception of the two engine air intakes (Tamiya parts B17 and B18), components from the Dragon kit were used exclusively. Since the fenders should be replaced by photo-etched parts from the Aber range, one has to cleanly remove the integral brackets from the kit's plastic parts. The gear cover with the two maintenance hatches (part C15) can then be glued. The projectile deflector in front of the driver's vision port was supplemented with five flat holes on the top by means of a suitable drill, and the small slits on each side were carved with the help of a scalpel. The large hinges of the maintenance hatches were carefully drilled out front and back, and the moulded closures

were removed and replaced by appropriate components from Lion Roar. On the engine deck, the moulded-on brackets for the tow rope, and the closures of the maintenance and fan hatches, were carefully removed and replaced by etched parts from Aber. With the attachment of the new brackets for the tow rope, one should make certain that these have a special position in relation to later versions, since the A model only had one 10m long tow rope. The hinges of the engine flaps were again carefully drilled out for finer detail.

For the conclusion of the work on the upper hull I attached the two air intakes from the Tamiya kit (B17 and B18). In order to prevent disturbing reflections of the bright plastic, these components were painted black on the inside with Tamiya XF-1, before the grating material from Aber was glued on.

Likewise, the insided of the upper and lower hull were painted completely in black before sticking both components together. At the vehicle's front some missing

welding seams had to be supplemented and some of the existing welds were refined. For this, pieces of stretched sprue were glued on to the appropriate places, softened with Tamiya Extra Thin glue and afterwards structured with a scalpel. Also some of the existing welding seams were partly detailed with the help of a soldering iron with an accordingly fine point. One should proceed very carefully here and only use a soldering station on which the temperature can be controlled. Since I wanted to represent the left headlight casing openly, I had to mill out the housing (part B25) with a round drilling head and thin out the sides somewhat. The headlight came from my spares box and was also drilled out. For further refinement of both headlamp housings, several parts of the Aber set were used.

The connection angles between upper and lower hull at the rear of the vehicle were now supplemented by etched parts from Lion Roar, and refined with screw heads from Calibre35. Additionally, the

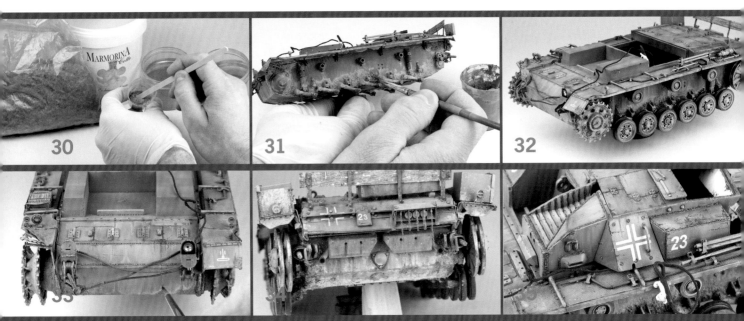

30 These ingredients were mixed to imitate dried mud. In the two cups on the right are different mixtures of ordinary soil. Nature offers an enormous selection of different consistencies and colours. I always have around nine different earth mixtures ready and always mix a little plaster and, depending upon the displayed structure, static grass and other materials. The last ingredient before the mixture is applied to the model consists of Vallejo Mat Gel Base. The advantage of this material is its absolutely matt finish. 31-35 The mixture was carefully applied to appropriate areas with an old paintbrush. A part of this earth mixture was strongly diluted with water. The resulting 'washing' was then used to blend together less-muddied areas. This mix can also be used as a kind of dust-washing on the rest of the model.

36

36 Here are photos of the completely finished vehicle, but without the figures. Besides the usual details which should give the model a vivid impression, I focussed on a specific arrangement of elements in certain areas, to attract special attention. Thus, the front of the vehicle was more emphasised by the mounting of the tow rope. The course of the tow rope directs the view to the left fender with all its interesting tool holders. The wooden railing and the various pieces of equipment shown on the engine deck also catch the eye. Over the replacement road wheel on the right side of the superstructure, one's gaze flows back to the front sprocket wheel without the coverage. In this manner, each side of the model exudes striking detail and one's gaze is accordingly directed.

cover of the inertia starter from the Dragon kit (part A43) could be installed. A last important detail at the rear of the vehicle, in particular on the version A of the StuG III, represents the un-armoured launcher for the smoke grenades. With the representation and refinement of this component one should pay particular attention. Mine was built entirely with photo-etched parts and soldered. The smoke grenades themselves originate from the Tamiya kit (parts A5) and only had to be slightly modified and shortened.

Fenders

This question arises again and again…whether it is actually necessary to replace the kit fenders with etched parts, especially considering newer generation models which come with a wealth of detail. But the fenders are a characteristic feature and an important detail, on which one can express the individuality and personality of the specific vehicle. For me, the photo- etched brass offered a more realistic representation of damage and wear, which wouldn't be achievable with a plastic part. Without doubt, the processing of photo-etched parts also means more work and thus a larger amount of building time. So, it depends on what kind of story one wants to tell with the vehicle, and in which context one wishes to represent.

As for working with PE parts I would like to focus briefly on the most important point, namely the connection of the metal parts themselves. Here, Superglue and soldering are valid methods. In my view, however, soldering is the best and only way to obtain truly robust connections between the various metal parts. Of course, soldering is more challenging than working with Superglue, but it is rewarded with a clean and stable connection.

Although the Lion Roar set is accompanied by a complete set of etched fenders, I still chose those from Aber. On the one hand, I have built this set several times and appreciate its quality and value, but on the other, detailing of individual components is much better when compared to Lion Roar. The work on the fenders began with the assembly of the connecting angles between the upper and lower hull. These were brought into shape with a bending tool and then soldered together. In more visible areas the components were further refined with Ca-

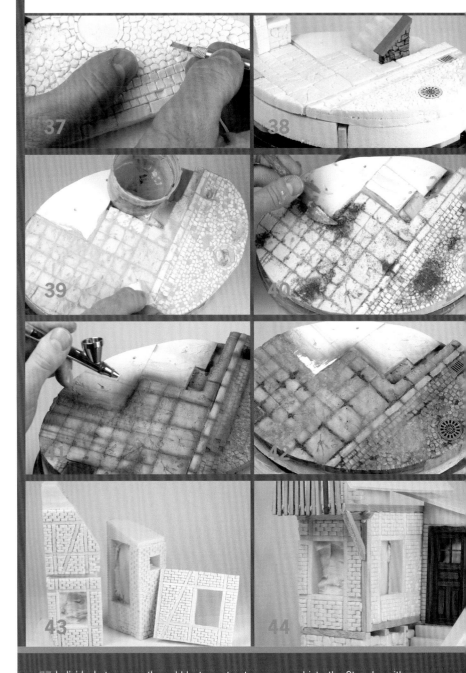

37 Individual stones on the cobblestone street were carved into the Styrodur with a scalpel. 38 The finished half of the base, consisting of a cobblestone street and yard. Further elements, such as a small wall and the stairs of the building, were likewise added. The laser-cut manhole covers are from Fredericus Rex. 39 All gaps were sealed with a thin mixture of plaster. 40 Dirt and debris were strewn in places and fixed with diluted white glue. 41 The base coat was done with Tamiya acrylics. 42 Subsequently, individual stones were post-processed with different filters from Vallejo. Vegetation and further dirt concluded this section of the base. 43-44 Construction of the buildings starts with an exact sketch in 1/35. From the sketches, the individual components of the building are cut out of the Styrofoam and engraved. Here, one should proceed in logical sections and construct the building not as only one component, but divide it into several sections. This simplifies detailing and engraving and, later painting. The door was built from scratch with several strips of wood.

libre35 screw heads. Then, the finished units were attached to the model with Superglue gel. The fenders themselves were built according to the instructions and soldered. Some of the planned damage was already created prior to soldering, while other examples were rendered only on the finished component. This ultimately depends on the specific parts and the nature of the damage which should be displayed. Before the fenders are attached to the model they still required detailing on their top sides. The very finely detailed tool clamps from Aber must first be assembled as usual from multiple parts.

These very small and delicate components were also securely and firmly fixed to the fenders with a soldering iron. The tools originated to a large extent from the On Vehicle Equipment Set from Tamiya, apart from the gun cleaning rods, which came from a Voyager set. Special details on the fenders are the two rear stowage boxes and the tool crate, both of which were completely made of etched parts from the Lion Roar set, and partly received random battle damage. The fixing of

the two front position lamps (parts B15) and the two circular rear lights represented the conclusion of the detailing on the fenders. Wiring, in each case, was reproduced with thin copper wire, lead wire and lead foil.

The casemate and the gun

Starting from Stage 6, Dragon's instructions deal with construction of the casemate. The area above the gunner, which represents the late arrangement of the two hatch covers, had to be replaced by component M9. The small front hatch was slightly thinned with a scalpel in order to achieve scale thickness, while the step-like representation of the bullet deflector before the gunner's sight (just above the driver's hatch) was sanded off completely, since it coincides with the original. During production of the A version, individually welded rectangle profiles were installed as bullet deflectors in to the viewing channel. I developed the new, more accurate viewing channel by thin plastic strips (0.25mm x 1.5mm) of Evergreen, and added small weld seams from stretched sprue. Good

scale drawings and original photographs were, again, a basic requirement.

After gluing on the front of the casemate with the driver's vision port (part A2), a few weld seams had to be revised. In particular, on the armour on the bow of the casemate, on which the sloped armour plates are welded, one can recognise thin weld seams in photos of the original vehicle. These had to be supplemented on my model. Likewise, the side view of the driver and the radio box on the left side has also been refined with weld seams. Over the radio box, two conical pins from the Bronco set were attached (mounting plate of the commander's telescope) and at the rear, the aerial mount was positioned in a slightly inclined position which can often be observed. The lifting lugs at the front are from the Tamiya kit (parts A28). According to reference material, the attachment of the roof on the A version was realised by recessed slotted bolts, not by raised pins as in the kit. Therefore, all moulded-on pins had to be completely removed, then, sink marks were carefully reproduced in the appropriate places with the help of a small drill. These were supplemented with screw heads from Aber's set 35A101. The commander's hatch and front loader's flap were again re-built with plastic material. In terms of scale, the original kit parts here are far too thick, which doesn't really matter if fixed in the closed position; with opened hatches, though, it becomes very clear. The hinges and locking mechanisms were supplemented from the Aber set. When attaching the rear wall of the superstructure (part C22) some columns suffered from poor fit, so filling was required. Additional armour on both sides of the superstructure (parts C17 and C18) was screwed on the original vehicle, and on the model were portrayed in the same way, with slotted countersunk screws as on the superstructure's roof. The handles were replaced with copper wire and their bases are from the Aber set. When gluing the two additional armour plates on the model, one should ensure

that the notches on the lower halves fit exactly over the carrier of the fenders. The superstructure itself was not glued to the upper hull, so that it could be removed again later for easier painting.The Sturmkanone StuK 37 7,5cm L/24 comes from Armorscale and consists of a turned aluminium barrel, with the complete cradle armour and gun shield made of resin. Both parts are of excellent quality and it requires only minor reworking with a little plastic material on the back of the cannon screen to ensure the etched parts from Aber fit perfectly. Also, installation of the gun was delayed to ease painting and weathering.

Modifications by the troops

In order to make my model more interesting, and to add well-used character, I made some modifications on the basis of several original photographs. Apart from the damage on the fenders and stowage

boxes, I also attached a railing at the rear of the vehicle, on the engine deck. This was created from remainders of a PE fret and a piece of lime tree strip, supplemented by screw heads from the Calibre35 set. On the additional armour on the right side, I attached a bracket with spare road wheel. The latter comes from the Tamiya kit and was accordingly drilled out and detailed. Due to the load on the engine deck, the tow rope was stowed on the vehicle's front, which can also indicate recent towing action. The steel cable comes from Karaya and was completed with the end pieces (parts A4) from the Tamiya kit and a tow shackle by RB Model. As often observed on early assault guns, spare track links were hooked on the rear towing horns, behind the mufflers (remnants from the Friul kit). The bulk of the load on the engine deck originates from different sets from PlusModel, and from the spares box.

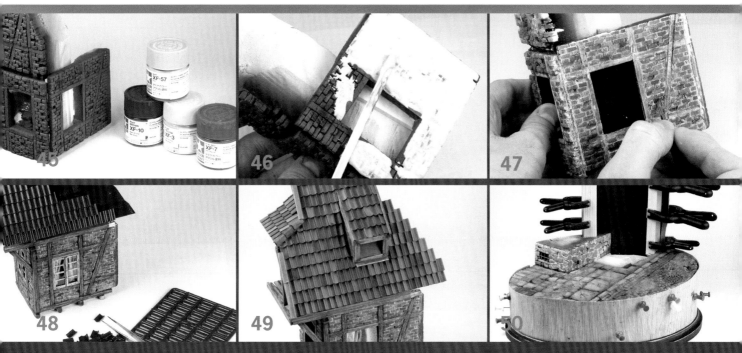

45 Painting was executed with and airbrush and Tamiya acrylics. First, a base colour in heavily darkened Hull Red. This was followed by the base shade of the brick wall. 46 Then, the brick wall was coated with a thin plaster mixture and, excess was wiped off with a piece of plastic sheet, so that the mixture remained exclusively in the joints. 47 Individual bricks were further emphasised with different colour blending, to ensure a more varied and realistic overall view. 48 The roof tiles came from miniature bricks by the company Juweela. These need to be glued piece-by-piece to the substructure; somewhat tedious work, but the end result is very convincing. 49 Base colour of the roof tiles, first again with the airbrush and, afterwards, more colour variations with the paint brush. 50 Oak wood veneer had to be adapted to the oval shaped base…not a simple task.

Painting

For a long time, the prevailing opinion was that all German military vehicles up to 1943 were uniformly painted in dark grey. In recent years, however, some outstanding authors have questioned this theory on the basis of numerous contemporary photographs, test reports and instructions. Around 1940, German military vehicles were not only painted in dark grey, but were also provided with a factory-applied camouflage finish. After reading reports of well-known authors (Culver, Zaloga, Jentz) I offer the following:

In the period 1939 to July 1940 army equipment was to be painted in the scheme of two-thirds dark grey and one-third dark brown (AHM 1937, Ziffr.340 and AHM 1938, Ziffr. 687). Only an army report of July 30, 1940 laid down any uniform colour application of dark grey. According to the excellent publication of Wolfgang Zimmermann and Peter Müller on the Sturmgeschütz III, the first 55 assault guns were ordered in grey/brown, according to the then valid regulations. That would mean that all StuG III Ausf.A (thus the first 30 assault guns) were painted in this colour. Due to the low contrast between the dark grey and dark brown, this camouflage is difficult to recognise on most black-and-white photographs. Especially when dust and dirt comes into play, the camouflage pattern can only be suspected. This low contrast could be why the camouflage pattern was rejected. A small experiment clarified why one cannot recognise this camouflage on many historic black and white photos. I photographed my model during the various stages of painting and weathering in black and white, and while the contrast was clearly obvious in the colour photos, on the black and white shots, the model looks almost monotone. Especially when dirt and dust is applied during the weathering, the camouflage completely disappears on the black and white photographs.

Base paint and camouflage pattern

By now, one should have had sufficient thought about the camouflage one wishes to portray, for example, with the help of drawings and photographs.

In order to get a better idea of how the camouflage will act on the model, and as an aid during the painting process, I printed side view copies of the assault gun. On these I applied the camouflage pattern with pencil crayons, which helped tremendously during the airbrushing phase, in which Tamiya acrylic paints were used exclusively. These paints were worked with light and shade effects during the application of the base coat, in order to give the model more volume and contrast.

Weathering

Rather than explicitly describing the weathering of this model, I would like to refer readers in this context to the StuG III Ausf. G mid-version (Farewell to the Faith). My methods and practises are fully described there and I would only repeat myself here. A significant difference, however, concerns the 'contamination' of the vehicle. Since the planned scene should take place in May, thus early summer 1940, here dust is the dominating element. On the basis of several pictures I would like to explain a few steps.

Chippings and rust

Since these vehicles were quite new and performed their first mission during the campaign in France, one may probably expect very little paint damage. This was my first thought, too, until I came across some surprisingly meaningful pictures during my research, which prove the exact opposite. I was quite surprised at how these vehicles looked after the first weeks of combat which, on the other hand, made me happy as a modeller since weathering effects really breathe life into a model. Nevertheless, one should hold back oneself with the paint chipping and carefully study the damage shown in re-ference photos; less is definitely more. What should not be seen on these vehicles is rust. Except for replacement track links, it's doubtful any components had long enough time to oxidise.

Soil and dust

I start applying the dirt at the lower hull with some thin washes of 872 Chocolate Brown from Vallejo. This layer is followed by further brown and beige shades, which I dabbed onto the surface of the model and then worked in while wet with the help of a damp brush. Here, it's very important to keep the surface of the model moistened during processing. Lighter dust layers were applied with Vallejo 837 Pale Sand and spread with vertical brush strokes in downward motions.

The figures

One doesn't always have to rely on resin figures! With Dragon's Gen2 products, the the difference in quality between plastic and resin figures has been lessened considerably. Not only are Dragon's figures well-detailed, there are also many

51 The finished figure of the ZB 26 gunner. Besides parts from an Aber set, lead foil and a few resin equipment pieces were employed.

52-53 Two infantrymen who later will be placed on the engine deck of the StuG.

54 The commander with the scissors telescope. I could recognise this handling of the 'scope on several original photographs.

55 The interested, listening loader in place.

56-57 Finished infantrymen. Here one can appreciate the amazing quality of these figures, any one of which would be great in a single figure-vignette.

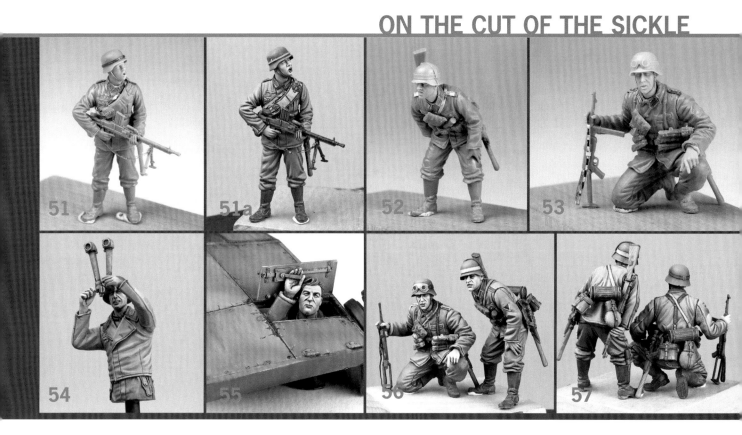

pieces of high quality personal equipment and weapons. I had the set 6281 Germania Regiment, France 1940 ready for quite some time and wanted to represent these characters in a small scene. Although the original plastic heads included in this set are not bad, I chose to add after-market heads from Hornet. Some of the poses were slightly modified and a few small changes to the uniforms were also carried out, since the figures for my planned scene should not be members of the Germania Regiment, but the Infantrie Regiment Großdeutschland. Three of the four characters from the Dragon kit were used for this purpose.

The two other (half) figures originated from my spares box. The commander with the scissors scope comprised a Resin Torso from Royal Model and new arms and a head from Hornet. The loader, with whom mainly only the head is to be seen, was constructed from a Dragon figure and a further Hornet head and a hand.

The allocation of figures on the base should be simple. The infantrymen discuss procedures on the basis of a map with the commander of the StuG III, whereby the loader is listening to the conversation with great interest. The infantryman in front of the vehicle both clarifies the dimensions of the vehicle, adds further focus with his impatient gesturing. As always, I exclusively use acrylic paints for painting figures. Initially, all parts were primed with the airbrush and Tamiya acrylics, and light and shadow effects were added. These nuances were then refined using a paintbrush and Vallejo acrylic paints.

The diorama

My planned scene should take place during the French campaign in May/June 1940, more precisely during the fighting around the city of Amiens. This small French town was on the so-called 'sickle cut' route on the way to the Channel coast and to Dunkirk. On May 20, 1940 it was conquered by the German Army. The area is more rural and thus one must include this condition among other things into the planning of the base. Therefore I decided to build a cobbled street with a typical half-timbered house as background. I have divided the construction of the base into two sections, once the street or the courtyard, and on the other hand the building. Both elements were created mainly from Styrofoam, which represented a new approach for me. The processing of this material is very easy and also the most complex structures can be created quite quickly and easily, and the finished components are very light to handle. Previously, everything had to be created in a tedious and time consuming manner with plaster, but now the appropriate forms can be created simply, cleanly and quickly from Styrofoam.

The cobblestones

Let's begin with the cobblestone street and the courtyard of the building. All items are made entirely of Styrofoam. First of all the rough shape of the later construction unit was cut out of the Styrodur board. Then the structure of the individual stones of the road was carved into the material. With the yard the individual stone slabs were cut and afterwards stuck piece-by- piece on the base. Then followed painting with an airbrush.

The building

I've always been enthusiastic for architecture in modelling and the exact implementation of these plans was always a challenge. From an artistic point of view, however, my preference has always been for old 'skewed by wind' half-timbered buildings with character, on which everything should be less than perfect … and one can let off steam in terms of painting and weathering.

After being inspired by countless original photographs and architectural drawings, I made several rough designs of the later model. After precise planning and production of accurate scale drawings for each section of the building, the actual construction could finally start.

The details

The actual base was created from Styrofoam and was covered with thin oak veneer. As it turned out, not a simple task with an oval shaped base! Most of the vegetation I designed with the help of various products from miniNatur, such as the ivy, the vine, nettles, etc. The wheelbarrow and wine boxes are scratch-built items, while the wine bottles and a few more details came from MiniArt set No.35550. After conclusion of all work, the oak wood veneer was coated with several layers of wood stain.

The finished Diorama

Without the editor this diorama would probably not have emerged in just four months. The StuG III Ausf. A had indeed sat on my wish list for some time, but only through working on this book did I take on the challenge.

Initially, due to time constraints, I planned to build the vehicle without the base and the figures, but my ambition and the urge to try out new techniques with Styrofoam led to this diorama. Ultimately I'm very happy with the finished result, since a vehicle model, without doubt, becomes more effective in an appropriate context.

Volker Bembennek

ON THE CUT OF THE SICKLE

BATTLE

Text and model by
Bernhard Lustig

German modeller Bernhard Lustig presents his superb interpretation of the aftermath of a battle on the Easter Front with this exhausted crew of a veteran Sturmgeschutz III Ausf. E

In my eyes the short-barreled StuGs are synonymous with the period of the Blitzkrieg and Operation Barbarossa, and the StuG III Ausf. E is the last member of that family.

Between September 1941 and March 1942, 284 Sturmgeschütze were built. The main characteristic of that vehicle is the large armoured box on both sides of the superstructure. Command vehicles contained radio equipment, while the others were able to carry six additional rounds. The installation of the large armoured boxes meant that the track guards had to be re-designed. It was also the first model equipped with a MG 34 for self-defence. In 2005 I visited the Motor Technica Museum in Bad Oeynhausen, Germany, where one can see the only existing vehicle. It was found in 1991 in a lake near St. Petersburg, Russia. Sadly, the vehicle is still unrestored and in a bad condition. The hull roof is missing, so one can see much of the interior. In some areas the original colour is still visible.

I loved that vehicle and said to myself that at some stage I would have to build it in model form. Unfortunately there is still no adequate scale example on the market but Dragon has announced the E-version for the near future. In spring 2011 I decided not to wait for this kit, but instead, I decided to combine an old

Dragon StuG III Ausf. F with a modern Dragon kit of the StuG III Ausf. G. In my opinion it was the best choice, because the older Dragon offering contained all I needed for a E-version. Because the kit is now more than 15-years-old, many parts of the excellent later StuG III are a welcome addition to that.

There is a large slot for the gunsight, so one has a good view of the interior, which is completely missing in the F-version kit. So, I knew very early on that I had to add an interior. The G-kit has a partial interior, but only a few components can be used for it. The lower hull of the G-version is really well done, but one has to cut the towing holds and reduce the length of the side panels at the rear ends, and replace them with parts from the F-version. The E-model had 50mm frontal armour, so I had to replace parts of the frontal armour with plastic sheet to simulate the correct thickness.

Interior assembly

The main parts of the upper hull were taken from the old Dragon kit. I cut all the screws and replaced them with small screw heads from Aber. The main work on that part of the vehicle was to re-design the gunsight slot and to correct the frontal armour behind the gun shield. The kit's parts in that area are over-simplified. Marks alluding to the correct dimensions of the gunsight slot can be found inside the roof.

Fortunately one can find good references of the interior in several books. The best pictures I found were in the Sturm und Drang book no. 2, Groundpower No. 07/2000 and 10/2000, the Armour PhotoGallery and Wireless for Wehrmacht. Many references I know, but these were necessary to build it as accurately as possible. I took the floor and the gun table from the G-kit, and the firewall had to be changed at the left corner.

The gun itself is completely different to the longer 7.5cm StuK 40. I took parts from an old StuG III Ausf. G update kit from Tank Workshop/Ordnance Models and converted it with plastic card, copper wire and putty. Ammo racks were taken from the Aber kit, made for the Tamiya StuG III Ausf. B, and they were perfect for the E-interior. Ammunition from Voyager was also added. The driver's compartment came from CMK and fitted to the model without any problems; the radio-equipment is also from Aber. The plastic sides of the armoured panniers are too thick for installing the radio-equipment, so I had to reduce them with a mini-drill for a better fit. The more parts one adds to

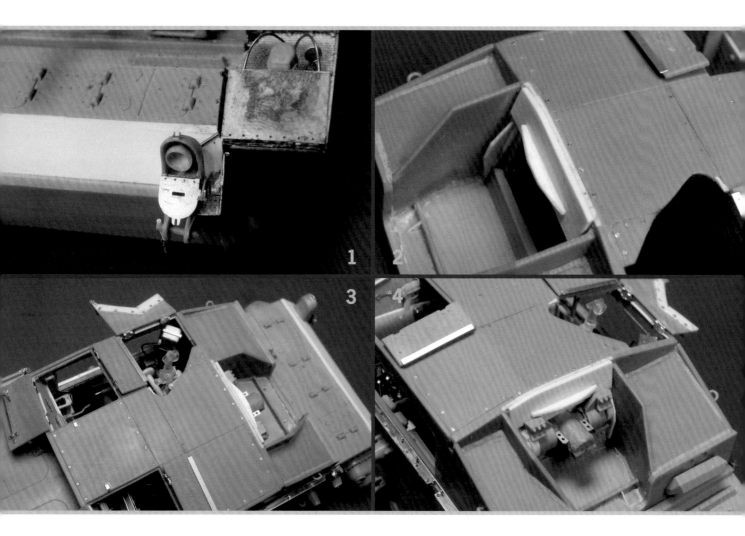

1 The welded seam is made from stretched sprue. The armoured cover for the headlight is the reworked kit-part, with a Royal-Model headlight and parts from ABER. **2** The frontal armour behind the gunshield has to be reworked. Welded seamlines were made of Magic Sculpt and the help of a rubber-brush. Please note the larger, redesigned gunsight slot. **3** Three large hatches are big enough to see lots of the interior. **4** Without replacing the frontal armour, the installation of the detailed gun is impossible. **5** The antenna-protectors received a additional mount, made from lead-wire. Characteristic for the early version are the hatches without air intakes. **6** The correct Ausf. E lifting hooks were found in the ABER set, and from the Dragon Elephant kit.

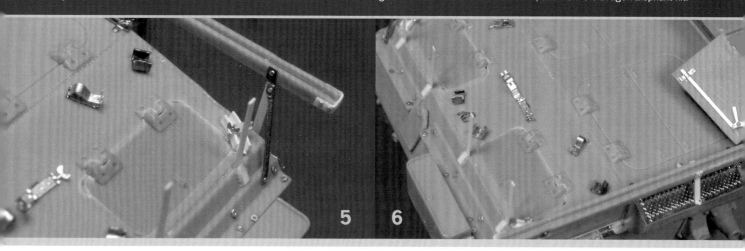

the fighting compartment, the more one can appreciate the very limited space inside the vehicle. So, it's absolutely necessary that everything fits perfectly. Endless dry-fitting was the only answer.

Completing the hull

After a seemingly never-ending period of building the interior, it was time to add the fenders and all the small details placed on them. In my eyes the Voyager etched metal fenders are excellent, but one has to handle them with care because of the weak material. Several units issued protectors to the width marker lights on both fenders, to avoid damage from branches etc. Several types of these additions can be seen; I re-created them with copper wire soldered to the fenders.

Painting begins

I always start painting with a black basecoat. The interior is painted in a 'broken' white colour, mixed from Tamiya XF-2 Flat White with a few drops of Flesh (XF-15) and Buff (XF-57). The floor is painted in a light blue colour. Before I started weathering the interior, I added a layer of Tamiya Clear to give a good base for the Fingerprint Decals, which are of excellent quality. To protect the decals from the following washes, a layer of matt varnish followed. The whole interior received a subtle wash with oil colours (lasur oxydorange/ lasur oxydbrown/ black), followed by pin washes, mostly along edges or areas close to the floor. After a drying period of 24 hours chipping can start. The best source for a good chipping result is a good brush. I always use Winsor & Newton Series 7 brushes (00), in combination with various oil colours (black/ translucent orange oxid/burnt umber) thinned with white spirit. I added some small personal items to the interior to give it more life. The small cigarette packets I got from my friend Kazue Yoshioka. The 'Signal' magazine is a download from the internet which is reduced in size and printed on thin paper.

The most interesting moment came when needed to be glued together. At this stage one can see if all that test-fitting was done properly. Not fixing the armoured boxes was really helpful in obtaining proper mating. Two headphone sets were the last things I added to the interior, before I closed the hatches with Tamiya tape.

I added all the small tools to the fenders and gave the whole model an overspray with Citadel Chaos Black. The base colour is Tamiya German Grey with some drops of clear varnish. Highlighting by way of a cloudy overspray followed, as one can see in the pictures. As with the interior washes, oil paint helps to blend the colours. Pin washes with dark oil colours provide more depth to the model. For accentuating the higher areas I relied on very gentle dry-brushing.

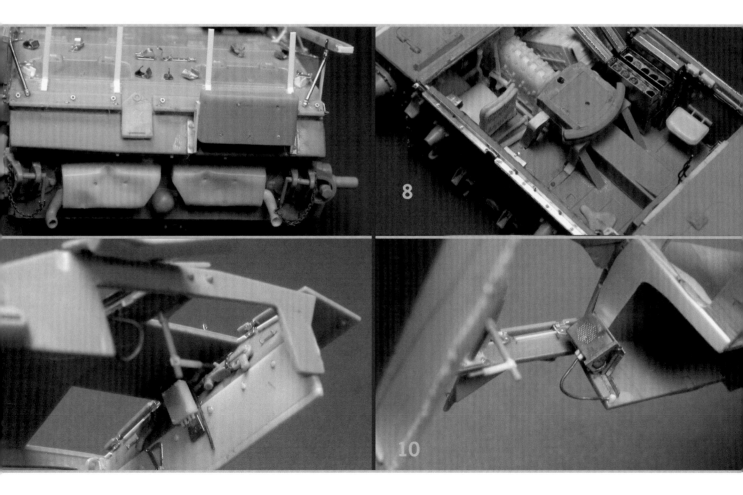

7 The damaged exhausts from CMK . **8** There are five containers (5 rounds each) stashed on the right floor. 2 additional containers are included in the upper right corner of the superstructure (3 and 4 rounds) So the STUG was able to carry 44 rounds of ammo. Maximum of 50 without the additional radio-equipment, which was carried in command vehicles. The commander´s seat is scratchbuilt. Personal equipment is placed at the left lower hull. **9** The rear wall including two MP40s. **10** The loudspeaker is included in the tank-radio-set from ABER. It´s located in a very prominent place, so it will be a eyecatcher in the completed model. **11 & 12** The clear plastic periscope was taken from thc Dragon StuG III Ausf. G kit. The leather bag for catching the spent shell casings has to be build up completely new. First, I soldered a frame from copper wire and covered it with rolled out Magic Sculpt.

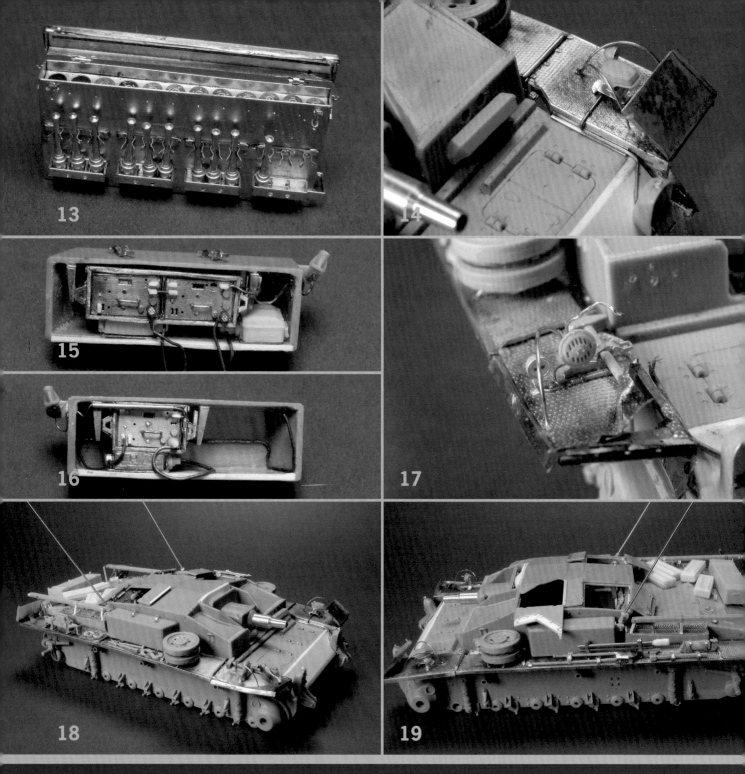

13 The ammo rack for 12 rounds is mounted in front of the rear wall of the fighting compartment. The stick grenades came from RB Models. 14 & 17 Close up of the front hinge detailing. A main difference between a C/D-version and the Ausf. E are the smaller hinges at the inspection hatches. Note the subtle and realistic damage inflicted upon the PE fenders. 15 The FU5 a unified radioset consists of Ukw.E.e receiver, 10 W.S.h transmitter and UKW E.h. Here you can see the right pannier. Don´t forget the wiring to the antenna-mount. I recommend to fix the armoured boxes to the super-structure last. 16 The UKW E.h. is located at the left pannier, close to the commander. 18 & 19 Note the sparewheels fixed in front of the armoured boxes. Everything is in place now, but at this stage not finally glued together. 20 After a black basecoat (Chaos Black by Gamesworkshop), a layer of "broken" white was added, before the floor is painted in a light blue colour. 21 Micro-set fwas used or applying the decals. 22 Many layers of washes simulate the heavy worn areas at the floor. Translucent Orange Oxid-oilcolour is a transparent colour and is my favourite choice for rusty areas. 23 The personal equipment gives colour an life to the interio and attention was paid while painting it, because of the large hatches so you will see so much of it! The large ammo box is my favourite item of the ABER-interior-set.

AFTER THE BATTLE

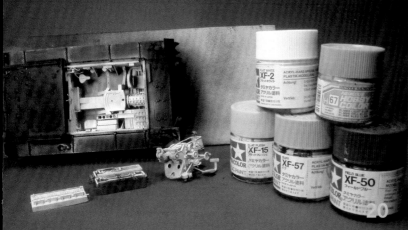

24 The author's personal favourite is from the Miniart range, in combination with an Alpine Miniatures head. **25** The other crew figures are a combination of parts from several figures, refined and converted with Magic Sculpt. All the heads came from Hornet. **26** Like the StuG model, the figures also got a primer coat of Chaos Black, here decanted from the aerosol can for use with an airbrush.

After this process the most time consuming work begins…micro-chipping. I tried several brushes for this, but Winsor & Newton Series 7 brushes worked best. I mixed different oil colours on a white tile and added a minimal white spirit for dilution. A different mixture gives a variation in colour.

Building the figures

I had the intention to represent a totally exhausted tank crew immediately after a hard fight, so I combined parts of several figures. Some individual components were built with Magic Sculp. Like the vehicle, the figures also received a black base colour. First I painted the face with Humbrol enamel, then the uniforms in Vallejo shades.

Last steps - the groundwork

From the beginning, it was clear to me that just a piece of groundwork with some grass on it wouldn't be interesting enough.

Adding a building would initially keep the eyes of the viewer away from the main elements – the StuG, with its interior and exhausted soldiers in front of it. A trench just in front of the main subject gives more depth and alludes to what happened just before that scene. The hasty Russians shot their last round at the German StuGs before they evacuated their defence lines. In my eyes it's easier to produce a muddy road or a building than to build a realistic piece of grass!

First I cut a piece of Styrofoam followed by a layer of clay which can be formed easily. I then pressed all the figures and the vehicle into the clay. After one day, the clay had dried completely, so I added a mixture from earth, small stones, wood glue, MIG Productions pigments (Europe Dust/Russian Earth). This was all blended with water and applied to the base with an old brush.

The grass came from Noch and Silhuet-

te. Small roots and natural pieces I found in the forest (such as moss) were added to break up the monotone look. I always start painting the groundwork with dark colours, which are gradually lightened in thin layers. Base colour: Tamiya XF-1 Flat Black/ XF-10 Flat Brown. Highlight: Tamiya XF-20 Medium Grey/ XF-57 Buff/XF-49 Khaki. Blending: Tamiya XF-19 Smoke.Several oil colour washes (Raw Umber/ Black/ Burnt Umber) give a natural look to the earth tones, while the grass got an overspray with various green colours, lightened with yellow-green.

Conclusion

I decided to build a 'perfect' model with all the items I could buy for it, and I must say that there were a great many small products used to produce a model such as this. But for me it was the realisation of a long-held dream.

Bernhard Lustig

27 As always, the model and figures were painted with a black basecolour and Chaos black from Citadel is a gret source for it. A Quick-wheel-tool was used when painting the first layer of dark grey. **28** The first layer is simply Tamiya Panzergrey (XF-63) with a few drops of Clear varnish and lacquer thinner. For all the painting, a Hager & Steenbeck Infinity Airbrush (0.2mm). was used **29** First highlight is a mix of Field Blue, Flat Blue, and again some drops of clear varnish. **30** For the second and third highlight I added Light seagrey and white to the first highlight. More white is needed for the third highlight. There is no highlight at the hatches! **31** After the washing / pin-washing-process a very gentle drybrushing helps to accentuate the higher details. Mixing a small amount of Rembrandt Permanent Madder Deep-oil paint to the Sepia and Burnt Siena-oil paint, gives the effect of the red primer. **32** Chipped paint at the fenders are done with brighter grey-colours. The wooden parts got a basecolour with Humbrol Matt 94 (dark sand) followed by thin layer of Sepia/Burnt Umber-oilcolour. The baremetal ends are painted with Alglad (dark Aluminium / white aluminium). **33** The excellent damaged exhausts are painted with the help of the "Rust&Dust"set from Lifecolour. **34** All the chipping is done now and the STUG is waiting for the dust and mud.

AFTER THE BATTLE

35 The mud is a mixture of plaster, earth, static grass and AK-Interactive wash colour (Kursk Earth).

36 Several heavy washes have to follow with various sand-colours to get a good result. Oilstains were then simulated with AK-Interactive (Engine-oil).

AFTER THE BATTLE

37 The Friulmodel tracks got a basecolour with Chaos-black followed by a various mixture of grey-brown-Tamiya paint. 38 The tracks got a wash with AK-Interactive (track-wash). To get a variation in colours, some tracklinks were painted in various colours. 39 Several pigments were thinned with pigment fixer and painted to the tracks. 40 The outside of the tracks got an additional layer of dust pigments. Lukas "Wischmetall – Silver" was added by a piece of cotton, wrapped around my finger.

AFTER THE BATTLE

41 Before the metal ammunition boxes are painted in a green base colour, everything got a "primer" in Tamiya Chrome-Silver, followed by a layer of AK-Interactive "Worn Effects". A thin layer of a mix of different green Tamiya colours follows right now. The green is rubbed off with a stiff brush and some warm water until you get the effect you like. **42** Clay was added to the Styrodur base. **43** The figures, and all the other small items are pressed into the clay before it´s not dried out completely. The sandbags were formed from Milliput. **44** The traces of the tracks were pressed into the wet clay by the help of vinyltracks from old Tamiya kits. **45** Adding some higher grasses brake the monotone look of the grassmat. **46** Note the harmony of the different colours. **47** Soviet 7.62mm MG Maxim Model 1941 came from Plusmodel. It´s a resin kit with some etched parts. The empty rounds were made of stretched sprue. The ammo boxes are from Miniart and Plusmodel. I drilled out the inner side of a Tamiya helmet and added some Magic Sculpt.

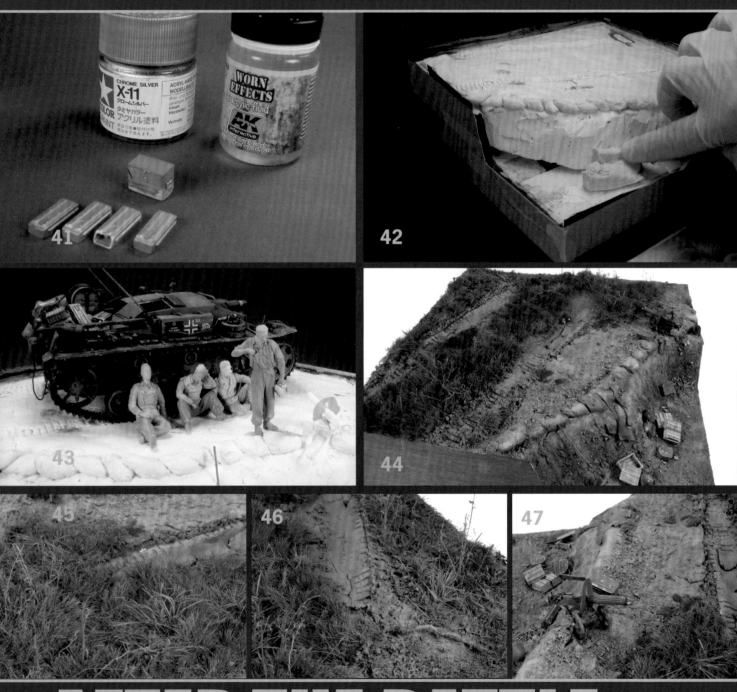

AFTER THE BATTLE

DRIVEN HARD

Text and model by
Michael Rinaldi

STUG III AUSF. B

American modeller Mike Rinaldi renders his StuG III Ausf. B as a more simple counterpoint to the other brilliant examples in this book. Built mostly out of the box, the finish is an extreme example of the classic white-wash over Panzer Grey.

When I thought about this project, I remembered there was one photo I had seen in the older Japanese language Sturm & Drang reference magazine years ago, which showed a wonderfully distressed-looking StuG III Ausf. B coated in a highly scratched and chipped whitewash somewhere in Russia, circa winter 1943. I immediately decided I would build that StuG for this book when I was asked to participate. Typically, I am not one to dive deep into a unit's history, or go into heavy detail to depict all of the elements present. Obviously, I don't model many figures, (or groundwork for that matter!), so my build would focus strictly on the model and the paintjob I would apply to it.

This gives the book a different perspective from which to present my model, in contrast to the other included builds. It is important as an effort to show you, the reader, various styles and points-of-view because not all modelling is the same and there is much to enjoy by simply focusing on the finish of a project.

The model
It was a fairly easy decision to choose the newer Tamiya Ausf. B kit release over the

The base kit is the relatively new Tamiya Stug III Ausf. B release, which is a good, if not a little simpler alternative to a new Dragon kit with noticeable missing detail. A couple of select choices from the Aber PE set helped to solve that problem.

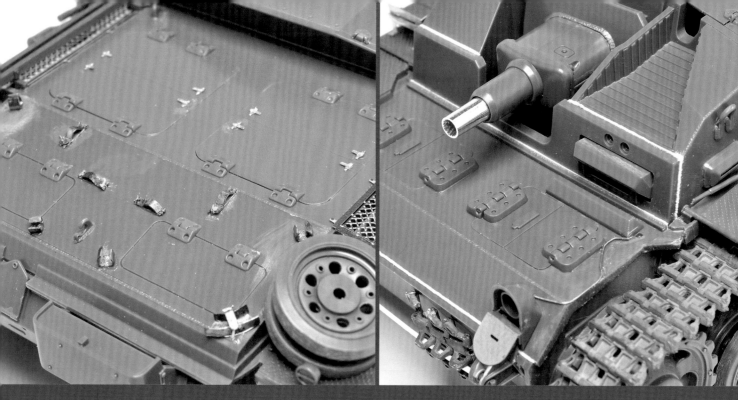

DRIVEN HARD

Much of the added PE detail is carefully chosen to enhance the base kit: the headlight and horn wiring, open front headlight cover, new weld beads, front spare track rack, missing tool handles, rear tow cable tie-downs, missing latch details and engine grille screens. The metal barrel and engine screens are from the kit.

---

older Dragon kit because, firstly, it assembles so much better and secondly, the detail is finer and more finely rendered. The Ausf. B also happens to be a subject not yet kitted by the new Dragon Smart Kit style of product, so instead I thought it best to utilise the less detailed Tamiya kit, enjoy the construction a lot more and, to add a few key missing elements to put it on par with more recent Dragon offerings. From that concept, I decided to add Friulmodel ATL-04 Pzr III/IV early 40cm tracks, (I had a set built from an unused older project already on hand), tool handles from Lion Roar and rear engine deck PE parts from the new Aber set dedicated to this kit. Also, as is common with my modelling, I used the technique of thinning the plastic parts to scale in many cases and here, I really put plenty of effort into the kit fenders. Some of Shep Paine's methods still work very well!

I had in mind a well-used combat veteran even more extreme than that in my reference photo, and I started assembly by lowering the front suspension a little for a more nose-down appearance; another reason to use this kit because its suspension is flexible via springs. I used lead weights inside the lower hull to set the desired height, then, added cyanoacrylate glue to hold the arms in place and cut the springs once dry so it wouldn't move (I removed the weights to fit the interior pieces afterwards). Assembly is quick with these kits, and most of my time was spent working over the fenders, showing heavy damage and adding new weld beads to the front end. My preference is for using thin styrene strips and plastic glue. It works a treat and produces very straight welds to properly look the part. The kit comes with a good metal barrel and engine PE screens, so I added those and cut some brass rod for the antenna. Missing details on the roof and engine deck were attended to next, and since I dislike the Tamiya one-piece tow cable, I added all the bits for the tow cable tie-down PE pieces from the Aber set. I used the kit tools and added PE handles only, which once painted look convincing from just a few inches away. A lot of this project was actually designed around that principle …'to look good from just a few inches away'. It would not be as detailed as a 'super build', but it was a decent compromise between a true out-of-the-box model and one wearing the full PE treatment. I left that to the other authors in this book to showcase those talents. My patience gets tested too much when I go PE crazy!

The basecoat

I will discuss the painting of this model in two stages, the first being the base colours applied under the whitewash. Luckily, with the time frame of the subject that means a basecoat of Panzer Grey. I would utilize Tamiya acrylics for this, but because I am showing a true veteran, I need to apply the appropriate chipping at this early stage of the process. I always prime my models and always use Gunze's Mr. Surfacer 1200 aerosol for its super-tight drying that provides the necessary protection for what comes next. The first colour to be applied is the red primer undercoat - Vallejo's Model Color Cavalry Brown mixed with Flat Red. I like it a little brighter when used under grey so it shows up better. Once it covers the model with the red, the first of many uses of the hairspray technique to achieve chipping and scratching occur. My brand of choice is Tresemme Fine Mist Men's hairspray, the subtle perfume smell adds to the experience! I apply two even coats from around 12 inches away, (let it dry in between), moving the can quickly but under

STUG III AUSF. B

The basic build is fast, with key adjustments to give the model a veteran's stance. The front suspension is lowered and, much fender damage is imparted onto the kit items. Thinning the plastic is essential to achieve this look and from there, many of the bends are done with a pair of flat-tipped pliers. The Friulmodel tracks came from an older project, which is why they already looked finished, but in fact, right after these photos, they were soaked in ammonia cleaner and stripped of the old paint to prepare them for a bath in Blacken-it, my favourite product for finishing Friul tracks.

1 The model is primed, first using Mr. Surfacer 1200. This protects the base colour from the strong abuse it will suffer during the weathering stages and, provides the right adhesion for both plastic and metal surfaces. It's cheap insurance from mistakes down the road. 2 The first colour applied is primer red, in areas where typical chipping will occur. Vallejo's Cavalry Brown is a great shade out of the bottle. 3 From here, hairspray will be applied, then the base Panzer Grey camouflage colour, ready to be chipped. 4 The grey camouflage is chipped because it will become a layer of depth to the finish, which is why this step is employed. From here the markings are applied and tools attended to. 5 After that, more hairspray. 6 Then, the whitewash can be applied. 7 Now the real fun begins and the white paint is heavily distressed, using the standard process of a brush, water and a little scrubbing and scrapping. This is also where the study of combat photos is important… constantly looking at references is the best way to keep the chipping under control. The goal is everything in scale!

DRIVEN HARD

control to ensure smooth, level coverage. It's all dried completely with a hairdryer before proceeding.

Next is the Panzer Grey. Using Tamiya paint, the mix is a 95% to 5% ratio of German Grey and Medium Blue and, a few drops of NATO Black. This gives a rich tone, with a hint of blue. I like the darker shades versus the popular lighter colours of recent renditions of Panzer Grey. Plus, the darker the colour under the whitewash, the better it usually looks. Once this is dry, which is as fast as the airbrush can be cleaned, the chipping process begins. All that's needed are a short bristle brush and tap water; I work in small sections, wetting the surface, before letting it sit a few seconds and then begin to work it to expose the red underneath in realistic chips. Because the grey is rather opaque, sometimes it is necessary to use a knife to cut away a very tiny hole and then start the chipping there, so the water can work its way underneath the top layer. The water does not dissolve the paint…it dissolves the hairspray underneath, causing the top layer to flake off in a very natural looking manner, which is perfect for our needs. Control is critical and, since just subtle red chips are required, this step goes quickly. Once complete, markings are added with Eduard spray stencils. Tools are painted in their appropriate

wood and metal colour, and the tyres are painted rubber, too. From here the model is looking half-way decent and is ready for the whitewash stage.

Applying the whitewash

To apply the whitewash, I must first go through the hairspray process again, exactly as described above. No varnish protection is applied, in contrast to many other modellers. I have never experienced any issues, but feel free to do so if you desire. For the white, I use Tamiya Flat White with a few drops of Gloss White and some Deck Tan. It will still look very white, but the tan gives it a more neutral appearance without the use of heavy filters, which I use less and less these days.

Chipping

From here on, the serious business of re-creating the extremely distressed whitewash takes place. It is critical to use quality reference photos at this point and, it doesn't have to be of the same subject, just the same type of finish you are trying to achieve. It's fine to apply wear and tear seen on one tank onto another, especially if the finish is more important than pure historical accuracy. Sometimes you can't find the right paint job on a particular StuG, but maybe on a Panzer IV instead. I do it all the time and this keeps the pro-

ject going without the need to expend tons of energy looking for a single 'right' photo. I have my one good StuG image handy, then a few others to inspire my chipping process.

Speaking of which, it really is about the feel of the stroke as you remove the white paint. Often, too much white will flake off so it is good to work in small sections. Use just enough water to see the chips start and then keep going until no more chips happen, repeat and move along. This keeps the resulting marks under control because the whole reason for all of this hairspray use is for scale accuracy. Otherwise, I would just use a sponge and be done with it. But the hairspray chips and scratches are far superior, very random and natural looking and, allow for superb linear marks as well as more regular chip shapes. It truly is here that the hairspray technique excels. It is nearly impossible to replicate these marks by any other method, even with a fine paint brush, without taking a very long time doing so.

While speed is not the primary purpose, using hairspray does create a good workflow that keeps the project moving along, allowing for a certain satisfaction level that I think is more important to a model's success than many modellers acknowledge. Nothing is worse than a model

8-9 Chipping of the whitewash is the most critical step of this project. I had to make it look like my photo; the marks must be in scale, and the process was slowed down to ensure it worked properly, but the results were worth the added effort. 10-11 Use of the pin wash is an important first step to the weathering, because it defines all of the moulded-on details. It gets the 'dirt' into all of the cracks and crevices early on, thus giving the model an authentic appearance. 12-14 The pigments are applied as shown, with the model on its side, the pigments mixed into three batches, applied in layers and then set at once with the thinner shown. Washes and stains complete the look.

8

9

DRIVEN HARD

14

that sits half-finished because the various steps take so long to execute and boredom sets in.

The weathering stages

With the main whitewash chipping completed, more standard weathering processes are applied. I always start with a pin wash and, in this case, it is a dark black-brown mix applied with a fine No.2 round brush. I also like to start some of the staining and streaking with this pin wash, because it provides some of the lighter tones for the stains. Darker stains can be added near the end of the weathering process.

With the pin wash stage complete, pigment application comes next. I start low down and place the model on its side, so the sides of the hull are horizontal. Large quantities of pigments are applied all along the hull, before being secured with a fixative. Once dry, the texture is very realistic and all manner of stains, leaks and splatters are then added to the dirty surface. I also attend to the outer wheel areas using less pigment, but the same basic process. The entire lower hull is treated this way until the right look is achieved. From there I begin to apply fewer and fewer pigments the higher up on the model I go. The tops of the fenders are given a light dust coat, with the exposed damaged areas receiving slightly more.

From here, oil paints come into play in what I call Oil Paint Rendering. The point is to really work every area of the painted surface to display the level of wear and tear one wants, or needs. The process is very simple: make a palette of oil colours similar to the base shades of the model (using cardboard scrap helps to soak up excess linseed oil and will aid blending), then with a selection of fine round-tip and flat brushes, very small amounts of colour are applied and blended into the paint. The general idea is to add tonal variations, shadows, worn edges and dirty areas all in one go, as opposed to using filters and random dots of oil in a less controlled manner. My concept means rendering the model's surface in the same fashion that an illustrator renders a drawing, providing maximum information to the viewer as a result.

Oils provide near limitless opacity and this makes them ideal products for this step; even better than enamels because they take longer to dry, allowing for maximum blending and effects. It is important to keep the amount of thinner used to blend each oil colour to an absolute minimum. I also use individual brushes for each colour. Do have a paper towel next to you and dab the blending brush first so it is nearly dry (99% dry), then use it to blend. Anything more than this and it will dissolve the oil into a wash and that is not the intention. I work my way over the entire model and, while it may seem like a lot, the results are impressive and truly worth it.

Now the model is coming together well, and I begin to tie everything together; all of the darkest stains, final pin washes to all of the hatches and, I go over the edges of the hatches with darker oils to reinforce their constant use by the crew…and so on. It is that time when your eye has to be critical to finalise the overall harmony of the model. I work a lot with assymmetry to add interest and a more natural appearance, so some areas will receive even more pigments and oils to complete the desired look.

Conclusion

I was very happy to participate in this, even with a simpler single model in a stand-alone setting. Groundwork and figures were left to other authors in this volume, as they do such an amazing job with them all. I also want to reinforce that there are different ways to tackle extra detailing and how a model can be presented. There is a pleasing balance with this project that showcases how using certain specific upgrades can make a big difference, without too much effort. From there it is up to you to apply the right finish and, as you can see here, a winter whitewash is always a very attractive choice.

Mike Rinaldi

This author has gone to great lengths to develop a simple system of using oil paints to render the details and history of a model's surface. The colours are complimentary to the model's paint scheme and to set it up properl, it is best to create a palette from scrap cardboard as shown here. This soaks up excess linseed oil and allows the oil to dry faster, properly matt and makes it much easier to blend effectively. Within each small section of the model, place the appropriate oil colour on the surface and then blend it in with a nearly dry brush and thinner. The idea is to achieve a very dry blend that tints and discolours the surface, to show rust and dirt, enhance the chips, or add a myriad of stains and streaks.

STUG III AUSF. B

DRIVEN HARD

StuG III Ausf. G, 26 Panzer Division, Battle for Cassino, Italy, 1944

Radek Pituch was inspired by a famous wartime photo and decided to replicate the scene, set in the Cassino area in 1944. To give the model a suitable environment, a completely scratch-built house was created, capturing the typical Italian look perfectly.

Text and model by **Radek Pituch**

The Battle for Cassino, an important strategic area in the so-called Gustav Line, lasted from mid-January to late May 1944. In May the Allies transferred the 8th Army to take part in the expected final attack on the Cassino area. There were 14 allied divisions committed for the attack. As we know the areae around the Abbey of Monte Cassino was held by the elite 1. Fallschirmjager division but it received orders to fall back before the Abbey was bombed to ruins. Before all this hap-

pened, General von Vietinghoff ordered two German divisions, the 26. Panzer and 29. Panzer Grenadier, to cease contact with the advancing British 8th Army and to pull back to the northern area, towards Rome. The 26. Panzer Division was stationed near Cassino, and it was the only German armoured unit to be committed in the battles in May in this area.

Inspiration was found in a photo of a destroyed StuG III G in a Militaria volume about the StuG III/40 family. Ap-

parently, it was taken after the Cassino battles in May. After beginning to dig for information I realised that the most likely unit operating with StuGs in the area would have been the 26. Panzer Division; this was my starting point. Having the photo as my prompt, I located the scenery of my diorama in an abandoned vineyard.

I wanted to portray the StuG slowly advancing among the shelter of buildings, when it broke down and the crew had to disable its gun. The vehicle was finally

IWM 015178

spotted by Allied tank crews who delivered two direct hits on the glacis plate, which penetrated it, causing an internal explosion of the ammunition. The most visible examples of damage to the vehicle were the blown-off collar of the mantlet and right-hand appliqué armour of the superstructure, along with damaged suspension. Careful study of the photo revealed that the vehicle sat tightly to the ground, most likely due to having its torsion bars broken. Further analysis of the photo proved that there was light visible through the bolt holes in the superstructure, so it was likely that the whole roof of the fighting compartment was blown off. It was even more probable because the vehicle's ammunition storage was located on the right-hand side of the gearbox, and judging by the hit marks on the glacis at least one of the rounds penetrated deeper into the fighting compartment - causing the ammunition to explode. With all this in mind, I decided render slightly altered scenery, less soft ground and near a vineyard building.

The figures

Having the major layout of the scene ready I started with the figures, and these were created using Magic Sculp. The photo shows two British troopers in casual outfit. The leaning guy seems to be

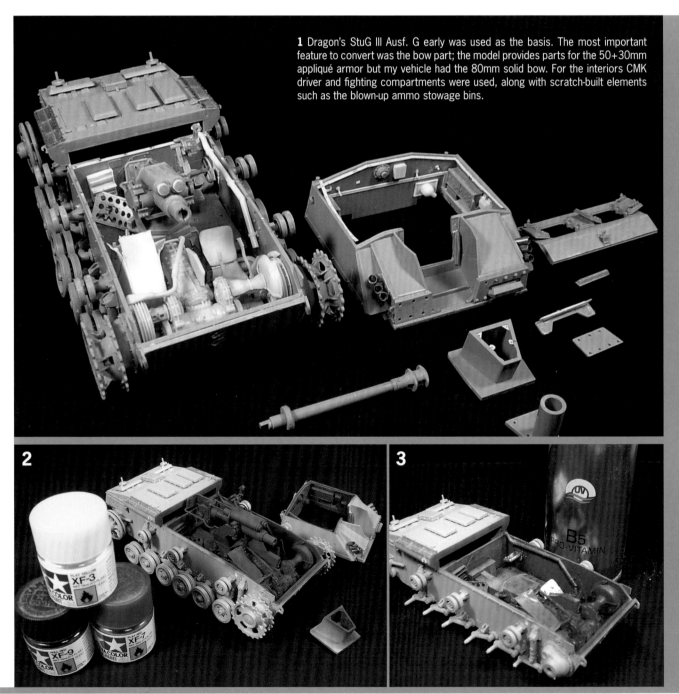

1 Dragon's StuG III Ausf. G early was used as the basis. The most important feature to convert was the bow part; the model provides parts for the 50+30mm appliqué armor but my vehicle had the 80mm solid bow. For the interiors CMK driver and fighting compartments were used, along with scratch-built elements such as the blown-up ammo stowage bins.

wearing tropical gear, while the second is outfitted with standard battledress. Moreover, the leaning figure is now available from Adalbertus brand, and I used one of the castings for my diorama. The second figure is totally bespoke and a commercial version of it will also be released. Both figures were painted using acrylics from Vallejo.

The vehicle

As for the model of the StuG I decided on the Dragon offering – StuG III G early version. The most important change was to convert the bow of the vehicle to the later solid 80mm plates, instead of the early 50mm+30mm appliqué; this was done with sheet styrene. Next, and importantly, was to convert the superstructure front

by driling holes for the appliqué armour plate that was blown off the vehicle. The model's gun offers almost a full re-creation of the 7.5cm StuK 40, but I needed to add details to the recuperators because these were visible due to the damage inflicted to the box-style mantlet cover. I also wanted the gun to be in a backward position (damage inflicted by the crew after the breakdown; a common practice was to remove the liquid from the recuperators and to fire a round so the gun couldn't return to its initial position, rendering it useless). Dragon's kit offers a basic interior so I was forced to use aftermarket additions, and the chosen items were

CMK's driver's and fighting compartment sets. These are good but need much attention when you want to build a vehicle with a destroyed interior. The exploded stowage boxes were scratch-built from sheet plastic, as well as the housing for the damaged radio. After the vehicle was finally built I proceeded with painting, and Tamiya acrylics were the chosen medium. I started with covering the interior in a red primer colour, then applying hairspray and white flat paint all over it. When it was dry, I gently started removing the white paint with a stiff brush soaked in warm water. As for the tracks, Friul's ATL 04 set (hollow horn) was used. These

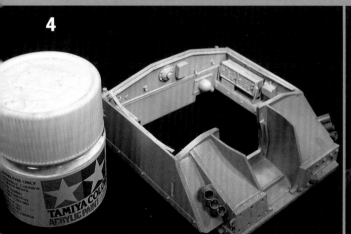

2 The interior was first painted rusty red, followed by a coat of clear varnish. 3 Hairspray was then applied over the painted interior… 4 …followed by a coat of Tamiya Flat White. 5 The next step was to scrub away the paint, with a thick brush soaked with warm water to ease paint removal. 6-7 Colour modulation helped make a monotone vehicle look more attractive. The first layer was Tamiya Buff, while lighter sections were painted with Deck Tan over the base shade. Shadowed areas comprised a mix of Buff, JGDSF Brown and a hint of NATO Black.

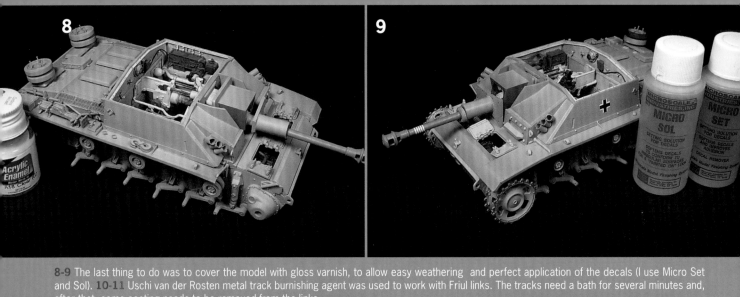

8-9 The last thing to do was to cover the model with gloss varnish, to allow easy weathering and perfect application of the decals (I use Micro Set and Sol). **10-11** Uschi van der Rosten metal track burnishing agent was used to work with Friul links. The tracks need a bath for several minutes and, after that, some coating needs to be removed from the links.

12 For chipping the vehicle, Panzer Aces Dark Rust is my choice; at this moment I also painted the inner rings of the road wheels with silver; these elements were always polished to bare steel.

were a common early type of 40cm tracks used in that period on German Pz IV/Pz III/StuG vehicles. These were blackened with the new Uschi van der Rosten burning agent, and were then weathered with a mixture of light sand pigments from the Vallejo range, mixed with water and plaster. One of the features of my StuG was additional protection of the superstructure by spare track lengths. These were weathered with Vallejo paints – a light mud colour from the Panzer Aces range. In terms of decals, just German national Balkenkreuz were applied with Micro Set and Sol solutions.

The vehicle depicted on the wartime photograph sports a monotone paint scheme of Dunkelgelb, so typical for German vehicles operating in Italy. It is not an easy to create a vehicle painted only in one colour and have it look interesting. The remedy came by way of the Colour Modulation process. Highlighting and shading different panels and surfaces of the model, in different tones of the same base colour, created a realistic and interesting overall appearance. Adding further filters helped to tone down the paint but still left plenty of diversity in the base colour shades. With German vehicles, I mostly paint them using Tamiya Buff for the base, and then modify it using Deck Tan and JGDSF Brown colours when it comes to highlighting and shading; this model was no exception.

The building and the scenery

The building was to be one of the most important parts of the whole scene. As usual in my projects, I wanted to obtain originality and that was the reason I decided to scratch-build it. First I casted plaster plates and then carved windows and door-

13 Plaster castings were made to assemble parts for the building. The stairway was created with foam described in the text, with the addition of a plaster cast of the side wall. **14** To carve the stone wall I first used a thick needle **15** To add a three dimensional look to the brick and stones they were sculpted further with a sharp blade. This is a hectic job but the effects are fully worth the involvement and patience needed

16 I smear the thin plaster on the walls with a simple spatula to create a scruffy, old finish on the building, just like it was built many years before the story takes place. This is a typical feature of old Italian buildings which can be viewed when visiting the country.

17 Construction is now finished and primed with Tamiya Deck Tan to protect the surface and, to strengthen it before proceeding to paint job and further weathering.

18 To create simple tufts of grass I apply some wood glue onto plastic card. **19** Then, using tweezers, I apply and form static grass; it's important to shape the tufts properly, so that the grass won't be too flat. **20** When the glue sets I use an airbrush for coloring the tufts, then simply detach them from the plastic card (wood glue doesn't stick well to plastic, but it is firm enough to allow easy painting). **21** Then, the tufts are glued to the groundwork in a random fashion.

22 Although the climate is dry in Southern Italy, I added lichen glazes to some of the roof tiles, to add further weathering. To do this, a three-colour mix of Vallejo paint was used (for the base coat, lime was ideal). It's important to dilute the paints to create a thin, transparent layer. **23** The effect was applied randomly. **24** A mixture of Vallejo pigments was used to further portray the dusty environment of Southern Italian soil.

ways in them. The idea was to build a typical one-floor Italian farm house – casolare as the Italians call it. A distinctive feature of these buildings is the use of sandstone as the basis for the walls, with additional bricks around the doorways and windows to reinforce these areas. And so I carved stone walls in prefabricated castings. A small cellar was added to the side of the building, attached to the stairway. As for the painting process I first sprayed several layers of Deck Tan over the building, then

adding MIG Productions' Neutral Wash to emphasize contrast. A further step was to add different shades of white over the scruffy surface of the plaster. This was done by applying several layers of diluted off-white base colour (a mix of Flat White and Deck Tan). When these steps were ready I painted the visible stones with a light sand colour and the bricks with light

red-brown. There was a need to add colours which would bring a lot of life to the building so the windows and doors, made earlier with balsa wood, were painted a blue-green, again a feature observed in Italian rural architecture. To imitate broken glass in the windows I used transparent plastic sheet, and cut it with a blade to give a realistic finish.

25 With the help of MiniArt's kit I added gear typical for a rural environment. 26 The worn paint effect on the door was achieved purely with a brush. 27 Close-up of the worn pain effects, achieved using a fine brush with a steady hand; weathering fluids were involved here. 28 Close view of the walls. The plaster effects, cracks and rough texture are evident.

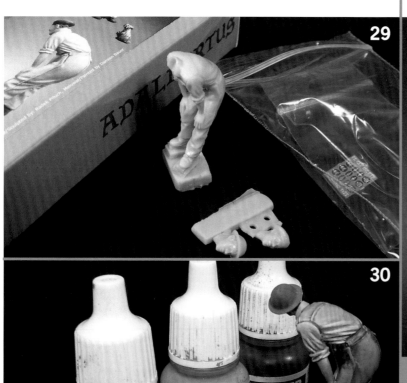

29

31

30

29 My self-sculpted 'Tommy' figure, now available from Adalbertus. 30 Basic Vallejo colours were used to paint the uniform (Beige, with Afrika Korps and Black Highlights). 31 A casual and relaxed-looking figure, as seen in the wartime photograph.

The scenery was to be simple - dusty, scorched-by-the-sun groundwork surrounding the building, with a little grass and other vegetation. My visits to southern Italy provided an impression of dry countryside and I wanted to show this in my scene. The building, as mentioned before, was to be an abandoned vineyard house so I needed to add elements indicating the use of the whole complex. An ideal solution came with the appearance of MiniArt's kit comprising wine bottles, crates, wine barrels and other useful diorama items. I also added a chair from an old Tamiya figure set and other small details such as a rusty bucket lying beside the wall, and damaged wooden planks.

The final stage was to put all the elements together, glue the figures and the model in place and add final touches to the whole diorama. One of the most important jobs is to harmonise everything, and that's why the pigment work on the diorama was left until the end. This allowed me to combine the model and figures with the groundwork, and to create a realistic scene happening somewhere in

Close view of the partially damaged fighting compartment.

Side view of the StuG. Oil streaks from the wheels hubs add an attractive look to the suspension.

Italy during the hot spring of 1944. Diorama building is a challenging enterprise but it brings much joy and fun for modellers. The most important thing when we want to obtain a convincing re-creation of reality is to find the balance between all of the things happening in the scene; these must work together perfectly when we want a realistic appearance. The scene shouldn't be too cramped and overloaded with details because they will be lost in the general view. As for me, one of the most important parts of realism in a diorama are lifelike figures because these bring real life to a static scene, and give the spectator a feeling that he or she is observing a moment frozen in time.

I would like to thank my girlfriend Ann for her support during this build and ultimately for her understanding. I would also like to thank Alex from Uschi van der Rosten for supplying his burning agent for metal tracks and the editor for inviting me to contribute to this publication.

Radek Pituch

JERRY GOT HIS!

Dutch modeller Roger Hurkmans recreates an emotional scene of defeat using a rare combat reference photo...but he wasn't the only modeller planning to re-create this scenario.

Text and model by **Roger Hurkmans**

What is the chance that two modellers could be inspired by the same photo at the same time? In my case it happened. I had found a picture in a book of a StuG III with wounded soldiers and posted it on a forum; immediately Volker Bembennek responded to this post with the message that he was working on exactly the same project. But because we have our own unique style and interpretation, the end result of our work would be totally different in the end, as you can see in this book.

I decided to make a StuG III Ausf. G from Panzerjäger Abteilung 54 during early 1944, together with wounded Dutch soldiers from the 4th Freiwilligen Panzer Grenadiers 'Nederland', located in Narva in the area Schotfeldlilienbac, where the Dutch lost many men during this fight.

By way of this diorama I wanted to depict an intense emotional impression of defeat, and I realised the idea by creating a cold atmosphere. The figures all look crestfallen and some are slightly, or even seriously, wounded. On the back of the StuG lay two soldiers who were killed in action and brought back from the battlefield to be buried later in a decent manner.

Finally, I added graveyard details to heighten the

air of depression; ironically, though, there actually was a graveyard in the area of Schotfeldlilienbach.

The model

For the StuG III Ausf. G I selected kit no. 6365 from Dragon, which came closest to the Abt. 54 vehicle I had in mind, and the kit is of good quality; like most of my models I replaced several plastic parts with photo-etched (PE) metal. I used the schurtzen and fenders from Aber, along with the kit's basic PE set. To make the finish complete, a barrel from Aber was added, with tracks from Friul and a brass barrel from Adler's Nest for the MG34.

Making the figures

From the beginning I wanted the poses of the figures to be as natural as possible. After I had built the base of the StuG, I set about selecting the figures and various parts that I would use, and ultimately, most were plastic figures from Dragon.

The time consuming part was setting in place the various arms and legs, and then filling the gaps with new sculpting by using Magic- ulp. I went in search of heads and hands, which were all sourced from Hornet. These are the best on the market and the choice is substantial. I sculpted scarves for most of the figures, and some of the troops were wearing winter trousers and I converted these to being un-tucked, to ensure a more negligent look (all this was also done with Magic Sculp).

I altered the rims of the Dragon 'Geuz' helmets by using a scalpel, and for the straps I used lead foil and replacements from the Aber range.

The base kit is Dragon No. 6365, with a host of details added from Aber's photo-etched metal range. Friulmodel tracks and metal barrel complete this enhanced build.

The reference photo that generated two dioramas for this book. The author has faithfully captured the quality of the event in all its fantastic detail.

DEFEAT OF THE DUTCH

The author greatly increased the story-telling factors by re-creating an emotionally charged scene of defeat by adding very impressive crew and soldier figures. These were all sourced from various Dragon plastic figure sets and then further enhanced with Magic Sculp, Aber PE details, and a host of Hornet heads and hands. They were then placed with an air of believability to further recreate the mood.

During construction, the author added many subtle, and not-so-subtle, nuances to the model. Note the added mud texture via real sand and Tamiya putty stippled on to the lower hull sides. The damaged PE fenders and schurzen supports are worthy of note.

The author uses straight-forward techniques to pre-shade the model, and then sprays a lightened dunkelgelb tone with Vallejo acrylics. Note how the colour gets lighter the higher you look.

Painting the figures

After assembling the StuG and the many figures it was now time to paint. I started, as per my usual method, with the figures. I painted both uniforms and faces with oil paint. If you paint using oils you must, however, begin with a good base of acrylic or enamel paint. This method has the best effect if your undercoats are approximately the same colour as those on which you will paint later, in oils (face: flesh tone, uniforms: grey, etc)

The undercoat must dry for at least a day before I start working with oils. As

an example, I will use the field grey uniforms. First, I undercoated the feldbluse using Humbrol 31, a mid- grey-green colour. After that, I painted the whole garment in a similar grey oil tone. I then removed most of the oil paint using a broad, flat brush; then I filled in the shadows; generally I use van Dijck brown for this. I always paint the lower part of the arms in an equally dark shade, again to emphasize the shadows. Then I apply the highlights by adding a little white on the upper parts. Then the blending process can begin. Oil paints are excellent

for weathering uniforms and blending in dirt tones on the uniform colours. I did this by applying some van Dijck brown or raw umber and blending it into the base colour. Another advantage of oil paint is that it takes a long time to dry, giving you a lot more time to achieve the look your desire.

The disadvantage, of course, is that you have to wait a couple of days after painting the rest of the figure. Once everything was completely dry (up to a couple of weeks), I airbrushed a coat of matt varnish to get rid of the characteristic sheen which is left

The author's exceptional painting skills are evident in these in-progress photos of the painted StuG and some of the figures. Smaller details are all given the same level of attention and the overall effect is harmonious and eye-catching. There is something new and interesting to find in each millimetre of this model.

by oils. For the collar patches and Dutch insignia I used Archer set FG35058. Finally I weathered the bottoms of the trousers, the boots and helmets with MIG Productions pigments.

Painting the StuG

Before airbrushing the StuG it's important that the surface of the model is clean and free of grease and dust. At first I washed everything using water and after that blow-dried the model using my airbrush. First I airbrushed the entire model using a dark brown paint. I always think this is the best choice for an undercoat as it's very forgiving later on as subsequent coats are applied, and for all those hard to reach areas. My main coat was a dark sand colour. I angled my airbrush above the model, spraying the paint at a slant to leave some of the dark brown paint showing through, leaving a natural shadow.

Then I sprayed an even lighter sand colour even more sparingly, using the same technique to give natural highlights. After that I sprayed a coat of gloss varnish and allowed this to dry thoroughly. Then the process of weathering can begin; I used a mix of indigo, van Dijck brown and Alizarin Grim oil paints. This mix provides a pleasing deep brown colour. I treated each panel separately and blended the oils into the corners. Pin washes were performed using the same colour mix. I always use acrylic paint for chipping, heavily diluted with water as this way you can paint on very thin lines. I think the chipping of a vehicle is an essential stage in realistic weathering, but you must never exaggerate it. Here and there I also added more highlights to the upper parts of the StuG using a mix of oil paint slightly lighter than the base colour.

The rubber bogie wheels were painted using a mixture of black and flesh (never use pure black) and afterwards they were weathered using pigment powders. The tracks were sprayed using panzer grey and afterwards were treated with different tones of pigments. Finally they were dry-brushed in black paint. This last stage

Close-up of the figures. Note how each figure have been converted and re-scuplted to fit the shape of the tank. A painstaking effort but worth every minute of work in the end.

4 SS Freiw

DEFEAT

added depth to their appearance. On the side of the schurtzen and the rear of the Stug I spattered some diluted raw umber and van Dijck brown to represent wet mud.

The base

I always like to create small scenes and try to avoid empty spaces where possible. For the gravestones I used an old set from Custom Dioramics, and these were painted in different shades of beige and grey. The brick wall is made out of plaster, while the structure of the stones is carved using a pulling knife. Stones on top of the wall are bricks from Plus Model. The wall was painted using red-brown paint and afterwards, diluted plaster was added to simulate the cement seams. Finally it was weathered using oils.

Gap filler was used to make the groundwork, using the vehicle pressed into the surface to ensure a realistic fit. Once fully cured, this was airbrushed in various tones of brown and grey. Leaves, trunks and stones were added and fixed in place using diluted wood glue. To create snow I used bicarbonate (cleaning salt), which can be proportionately added by wetting the area before finally positioning the StuG and figure.

The last thing I did was glue the nameplate onto the side of the base. I always get my nameplates from a UK based firm called Name-it, and it added a dignified finishing touch.

Conclusion

I immensely enjoyed creating this diorama. I worked really hard on the figures, trying to capture the right expression on their faces; expressions of anxiety and exhaustion. It was my most important intention to capture the 'Defeat of the Dutch' and their tragic struggle on the Northern front.

Roger Hurkmans

OF THE DUTCH

FAREWELL
TO THE FAITH

German modeller Volker Bembennek returnes to create a stoic scene of defeated German forces using the same rare combat reference photo as Roger Hurkmans did.

Text and model by **Volker Bembennek**

The Ausf. G was the last production series of Sturmgeschütz III and was produced in large numbers by Alkett and Miag from December 1942 to April 1945. During this time many changes were introduced to the production run, and experiences of the troops initiated improvements to the vehicle's performance and production methods. Details which distinguish an Ausf. G from earlier versions, or exact changes during the course of production, are not within the scope this article. Instead, I would like to concentrate on the specific features of this model, implemented by me. I opted for a Sturmgeschütz III produced by Alkett (Altmärkische Kettenwerk GmbH) during November 1943 to March 1944. The desire was to show all the corresponding properties and characteristic design of this vehicle.

Pz. jäg. Abt"Feldherrnhalle 1" Bridgehead Tiszalök

The Pz.Gren.Div. FHH had been stationed on the Hungarian Plain for refreshment and re-classification since September 1944. Part of the division was the Pz.Jg.Abteilung FHH with 28 assault guns. On September 28th the formation of an attack-group in the area around Debrecen was ordered, and was designed to beat back Russian forces west of the entrances of the Carpathians; the Pz.Gren. Div. FHH was part of these units. After weeks of bitter fighting, German and Hungarian troops, however, were to completely withdraw on the western side of the river Theiß at the end of October. The last two bridgeheads at Polgar and Tiszalök were abandoned on the night of November 1st.

I would like to show with my model a vehicle of the Pz.Jg.Abteilung FHH in these rear-guard actions. Apart from certain modifications, which according to original pictures were made by the troops, I would like to integrate several figures to support the scene and to symbolize the retreat. Great inspiration for the planned scene was gained through an atmospheric original photo, on which a Sturmgeschütz III served as a transporter for wounded soldiers. In my scene, the assault gun was to carry a group of wounded infantrymen back from the front line. The Major, pos-sibly the commander of the bridgehead, thanks the assault gun crew for its support in bringing home the men securely.

Preparation

The excellent Dragon kit (6320) served as a basis for my model, which represents a StuG III Ausf. G Early production, which would receive some changes implemented on mid-version vehicles. Also, the manufacturer-specific properties which clearly distinguish between Alkett and Miag production should be considered when planning.

Here is a list of changes to make on the Dragon kit to represent a mid-version machine produced by Alkett, from the production period November 1943 to March 1944:

- Zimmerit in waffle structure, applied by Alkett from November 1943 to September 1944 (implemented by ATAK set 35033)
- First and fourth carriers of the fenders were made of pressed tin, (Alkett from March 1943 to war's end (realized by components E4 and E5 from Revell's kit)
- 5mm armour skirts (early version with

mounting holes) mounted on angle profile brackets; used until March 1944 (Voyager Set PEA076)

- Railing around the engine deck, mounted by Alkett from November 1943 until the end of the war (part of Voyager update set 35121)
- Projectile deflector before the commander's cupola, attached by Alkett from September 1943 until war's end (component A26 from Revell's kit)
- Cast 'Saukopfblende' mantlet without hole for co-axial machine gun, Alkett October 1943 to September 1944 (Armorscale Set B35-031).

Mostly to increase armour protection and supply autonomy, many vehicles were improved and converted by the troops. Many of these improvements, particularly in terms of armour protection, were often quite dubious and only increased the total weight of already overloaded vehicles. A common example of additional armour was the fitting of spare track links on the front of the vehicle, and superstructure. Even the area around the commander's hatch sported track links for extra protection. But the structure of the track links meant that rather than being deflected, incoming shells were often retained in 'bullet traps'. Many of the factory-fitted tools and extensions on the StuG were also modified suitably by the troops. For example, the relocation of spare wheels on the rear of the vehicle to create more stowage space on the inside of the engine deck railing. Also the starter crank, or jack (which were quickly needed under certain circumstances), often got new, more accessible positions, particularly because they were hard to reach behind the armour skirts. In hot areas, with large amounts of dust, some vehicles were fitted with additional 'Filzbalg (felt) air filters. These tubular components (similar to Panzer IV Ausf.H) were attached to the left and right engine air intakes as an additional tool to clean the air for the engine, with the help of a Filzkartusche filter. A vehicle delivered in spring 1944 or thereafter, would have employed these devices during summer on the Russian steppes …another interesting feature for my model.

Assembly

Before starting with the first building steps, it was very important to prepare the resin Zimmerit parts from Atak and dry fit them on the model. This allowed correction of fitting inaccuracies at the outset, so that any errors would be avoided. Since Atak's Zimmerit was technically intended for the Revell kit of a late StuG III Ausf. G (and the Zimmerit was to be attached in a realistic way, some components needed to be re-worked. Zimmerit was only applied after the fitting of various components such as tool clamps, and thus would not cover the entire surface as represented by the Atak kit.

Apart from adding the resin Zimmerit, the lower hull and chassis were assembled largely according to the instructions. A few changes were still made, however, such as the removal of the moulded-on angles on the upper side of the hull, and filling of the pre-punched holes for the plastic fenders from the kit. These were replaced with photo-etched parts from Voyager.

Another detail that I wanted to achieve was the often observed 'heavy bow - nose down' look of the long-barrelled assault guns in some original images, especially if they were equipped with additional spare track links on the vehicle's front. Therefore, I first glued the respective rear-most road wheel bracket (parts B7 and B8) on the left and right side, and the rear shock absorbers. Then I removed the bracket pins of all the other road wheel brackets on both sides. The front suspension arms (parts B7 and B8) could then be fixed in a slightly lowered position. Once it had dried, the remaining elements of the suspension arms (parts B5 and B6) were aligned. The installation of the front shocks (parts B34 and B35) required a small modifica-

tion, as these were in a subdued state and therefore must be reduced accordingly. The rubbers of all road wheels were re-worked with a scalpel to mimic wear. All moulded screws of the add-on armour plate (D14) on the vehicle's front were removed, before this component was detailed with the corresponding component from the Atak set.

I replaced part B28 on the vehicle's rear completely, with the corresponding resin part from Atak. However, since this component represents the late version, I

4 To echo original images the often observed 'nose down' position was also implemented on the model. The installation of the front shocks (B34 and B35) requires a small modification, as these are in a subdued state and therefore must be reduced accordingly.

5 A look at the rear hull - the ends of both exhaust pipes were carefully drilled out. Edges of the resin Zimmerit parts were smoothed with Mr. Surfacer putty to get a smoother transition to the plastic parts of the kit. Also further damage was applied to the Zimmerit and etched metal parts.

6 The edges of the resin Zimmerit were re-worked with a small ball milling cutter, so that a soft transition was made to the actual surface of the model. Also damage to the Zimmerit layer was generated in this manner.

7 In order to prevent reflections of the bare plastic, the interior of the two engine air intakes was painted in a dark, rust-protection red mixture, before gluing on the mesh material from the photo-etched set.

8 Finished engine deck; the tool box, just like the spare wheels, got a new position in order to create more space within the railing. Both wer converted on the basis of original pictures.

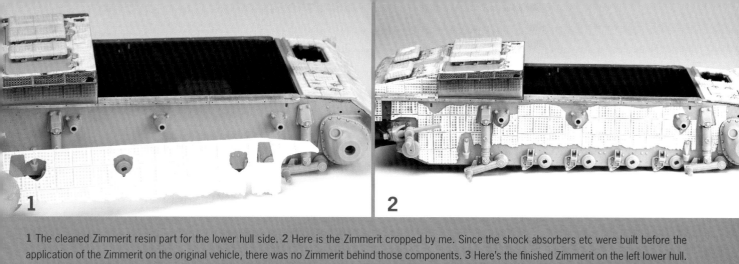

1 The cleaned Zimmerit resin part for the lower hull side. 2 Here is the Zimmerit cropped by me. Since the shock absorbers etc were built before the application of the Zimmerit on the original vehicle, there was no Zimmerit behind those components. 3 Here's the finished Zimmerit on the left lower hull. Since the original Zimmerit consisted of a hand-applied paste, the edges of the resin Zimmerit were smoothed with a small round drill tool. This achieves a smooth transition to the actual surface of the model. Also some damage to the Zimmerit can be added during this step.

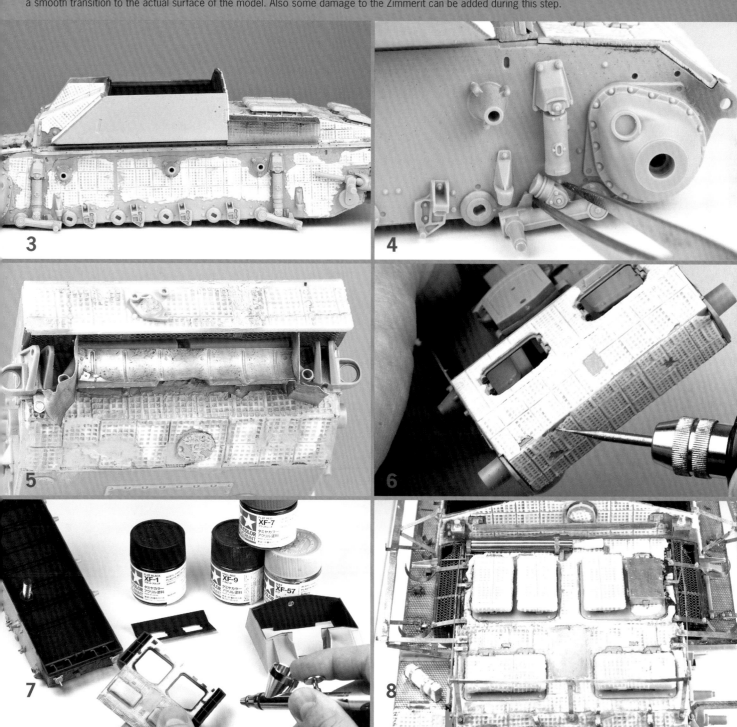

9-10 The driver's vision is included as a complete resin part in the Atak kit. I also added mounting brackets for spare track links from PE leftovers and round plastic material, and supplemented these with weld seams from Magic Sculpt.

still had to re-work some pointed screws, which were removed carefully from the original plastic kit part. The lid of the inertia starter (Part B4), I represented in an open state. I attached the mountings of the spare wheels (parts A18) to the left and the right on the rear armour plate. Further details on the rear hull were the addition of an etched metal air baffle for the engine exhaust, and the drilling of the two exhaust pipe ends. The interior included in the kit was used only in a rudimentary fashion, because according my plan, little of it would be visible later on. Only the floor of the fighting compartment and the gun mounts were used, as these were necessary to hold the gun.

Gear cover, enginge cover & the fenders

Additional armour (part D10) on the front half of the gearbox cover (part D7) was not required for my version. For the scheduled scene, the maintenance hatch on the driver's side was constructed open, and detailed accordingly. Then, the Resin Zimmerit was glued on. Instead of the Notek light for forward lighting, I opted for the installation of a Bosch headlight, was seen in an original image.

On the engine deck the resin Zimmerit was again revised and adapted to the kit. Above all one should remember here to cut/mill recesses for the tool mountings and other attachments (tool crate, mounting plates of the railings) into the Atak parts, since the Zimmerit should sit directly on the surface of the model. The armoured engine hatch covers and fan maintenance flaps were represented by resin parts from the Atak set, and replaced kit parts D9, D23 and D24. By shifting the

spare wheels to the rear of the hull, the parts for the fan flaps had to be slightly revised, so the moulded-on mounting plates were removed and some additional sections of Zimmerit (with a Zimmerit stamp and Magic Sculpt) were applied.

Before gluing the gear cover and engine deck to the lower hull, the entire interior was painted in matt black. After the connection of these elements, gaps had to be filled with putty.

The metal angles, which connect the lower hull with the upper superstructures, originated from the Voyager set for the fenders, and after soldering were attached with cyanoacrylate glue. Now, the model was ready for the attachment of the etched fenders. These were completely built from photo-etched parts, soldered together and in some areas battle damage was replicated. The connection of the fen-

Materials and tools for re-working of the weld seams. After I had carefully removed the moulded weld seams, I replaced them accordingly with new welds from stretched sprue. The projectile deflector before the commander's cupola originates from the Revell kit and, was supplemented with weld seams from Magic Sculpt. With the commander's cupola, I decided on a combination of photo-etched and plastic parts. The plexi-glass covers before the periscopes were made of clear plastic sheet. The hatch is completely represented from Voyager and is very fine, while the folding MG shield was completely soldered together from etched parts and copper wire, and refined with weld seams from Magic Sculpt and screw heads from Calibre35. The brackets and their components have, again, been entirely soldered.

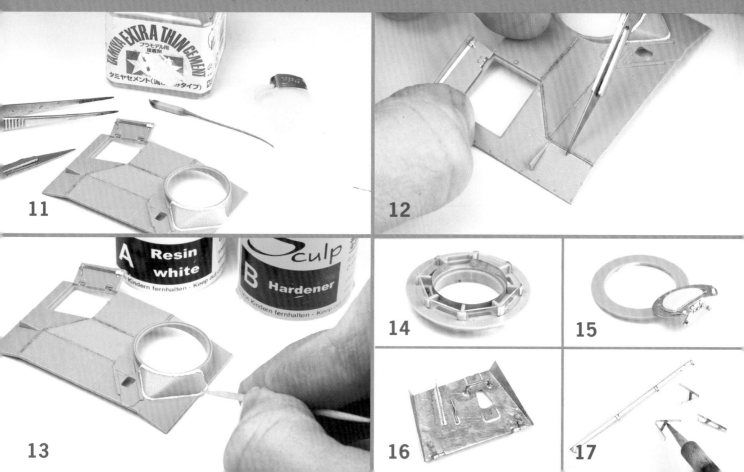

11

12

13

14

15

16

17

ders with the model turned out to be somewhat tricky, since there was only a very short time for precise connection of these units due to the use of Superglue.

The casemate & shürtzen

Dragon has represented the entire structure of the casemate with part C23 and only the roof and additional frontal armour, with driver's vision block, have to be added. The casemate was again fitted with the relevant Zimmerit parts from the Atak kit, whereby the driver's vision port comes as a complete resin part. On the left and right sides, as well as on the diagonal frontal armour, I added mounting brackets for spare track links from PE left-overs and some round plastic material. These brackets were additionally rendered with welding seams from Magic Sculpt. At the back of the fighting compartment, the standard spare track mounting was represented with the help of the photo-etched set.

Somewhat more complicated was the detailing of the roof, and here, all weld seams were revised. Although visually very beautiful on the DML kit, they are unfortunately too deep and uniform, and therefore incorrect. After I had carefully removed the moulded-on welds, I replaced these new versions made from stretched sprue. The projectile deflector before the commander's cupola came from the Revell Kit, and it was supplemented with appropriate weld seams from Magic Sculpt.

At the commander's cupola, which could be completely constructed by etched parts from the Voyager set, I decided for a combination of etched parts and styrene kit components. The reason was simple, in that the shapes and the material thickness of the plastic kit parts appeared more realistic. Also the periscopes from Dragon are much better in detail than the appropriate photo-etched counterparts from Voyager. However, what I missed completely in the DML kit were the Plexiglas covers before the periscopes. But in the PE set, the mounting

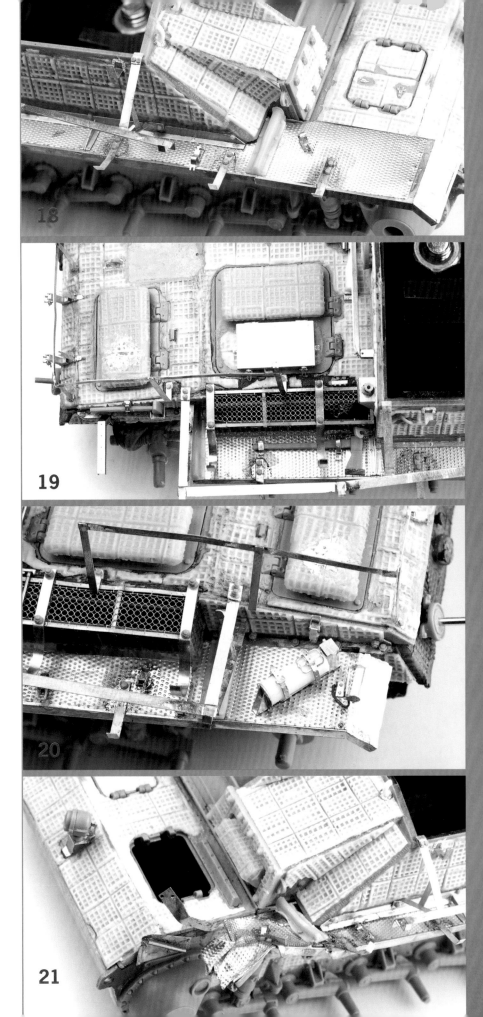

22

18 The brackets of the front skirts were supplemented with resin screw heads from Calibre35. Also, damage to the brackets was created. 19 Changing of the position of the tool box. 20 The lattices over the engine air intakes had to be modified somewhat, in order to be able to mount the additional filters. Also suitable mounts had to be supplemented. 21 Extra damage on the fenders.

23

FAREWELL TO THE FAITH

22 The additional 'Filzbalg air filters, which are attached to the left and right engine air intakes, were scratch-built in accordance with original recordings/drawings. 23 Relocation of the spare wheels, the mounts for the jack and the starter crank at the rear of the vehicle. Also noteworthy is the missing part of the right rear fender.

24 Pre-shading of all edges and recesses gives initial accentuation and volume. Subsequently, all large surfaces were provided with a primer in rust-protection red, whereby the darkest and strongest shade areas were left blank. 25 The first step of the actual base colour. Instead of a rich layer of paint, one should work with several highly diluted and cloudy layers. 26 By further mixtures of Tamiya paint and a gradual lightening of the colour, the highlights have been gradually emphasised. I always spray the paint at a slight angle from above. The higher the surface area of the model, the brighter it should be. 27 By post-shading all edges and shadows, one can achieve a beautiful contrast between individual areas.

plates are contained and the transparent parts were made of clear plastic sheet. The hatch cover was from Voyager and was very finely detailed…even the padding on the inside is included as a resin part.

The gunner's folding shield was soldered together from etched parts and copper wire, and refined with weld seams from Magic Sculpt. Brackets for the armour skirts, and the skirts themselves, were created courtesy of an additional Voyager update set. As mentioned before with this version I used the early style of armoured skirts. The brackets and their components were again completely soldered to achieve a stable connection of individual metal parts. Especially with such sensitive and delicate components,

a clean and stable join is very important, particularly if one wishes to portray battle damage.

Accessories & figure mods

As mentioned in the Preparation section, I wanted to equip my model with numerous additions and changes that were made by the troops. Some of these measures were implemented fairly easily and quickly, while others were somewhat more complicated, but the extra details lend a model its own unique character and provide a vivid picture.

Painting

From February 1943 vehicles were provided with a factory-applied base coat of dark yellow. After some considera-

tion, I decided to produce a single colour machine, which had a light camouflage striped pattern on the side armour skirts applied by the troops. Also, the barrel of the 7.5cm gun was decorated with a hand-painted camouflage pattern.

To give the model more contrast and variety, and to underline the combat look, some of the armour skirts should be rendered with a different camouflage pattern and in simple sand yellow. Especially with the armour skirts one sees in original images, they were often replaced due to battle damage or loss.

Base paint & camouflage

When it comes to painting with an airbrush, acrylic paints from Tamiya are always my first choice. The thinning medium

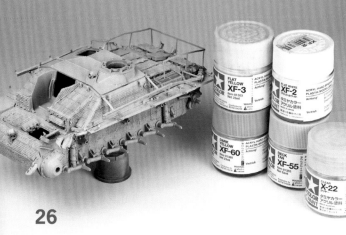

and degree of dilution is critical for success and a perfect finish. Tamiya paint is diluted with Mr. Color thinner in the ratio 1:2 and applied at a pressure of approximately 1.1 bar. With painting of models, I always follow the principle of light and shadow…so, the higher a surface on the model, the brighter, and vice versa. One can call this kind of painting Colour Modulation or Zenithal Light, but the principle is always the same:. The light falls on the model from one direction, in my case directly from above.

Weathering

For some time I have mainly used acrylic paint for weathering models. Unlike the traditional methods of weathering with oil paints, enamels and pigments, I try techniques such as filtering, washing and dusting with acrylics. This method has its pros and cons, but I personally am working more and with acrylic paint. One big advantage is that it can be diluted with water, but that may also be a great disadvantage, since these colours dry very quickly. The time water needs to evaporate, is the time it takes for the paint to dry! This means very little time to work with the colour on the surface of the model. On the other hand, the advantage of rapid paint drying is that one can apply many layers in a short time, such as when applying filters. Another advantage is clarity on the workbench, because one doesn't need different colour-mediums and their specific thinners, but only water, which also means no bad odors. Like everything, this method of weathering with acrylic paints requires practice and experience, but if one gets a feeling for acrylic colours, they offer great potential.

The figures

Even before I had started the construction of the vehicle, I spent a lot of time by thinking about the realization of an appropriate scene and its implementation. Especially if one wants to tell a story with a model or create a certain atmosphere, the inclusion of one or more figures is of great help. Only by the body language, the facial expression, gestures and possibly the interaction of the characters among themselves, is it possible to impart to the viewer the background and history of the displayed scene more closely.

Since I wanted to represent the retreat, the disillusion and the 'loss of faith in the victory'

FAREWELL TO THE FAITH

28 The camouflage pattern on the armour skirts was applied in a pattern of thin stripes. **29** The model at the end of the airbrush work. Individual areas were painted in a slightly different colour to achieve greater contrast. **30** The camouflage pattern on the barrel was painted by brush. A template was created from an original image of a Panther Ausf. A; the otherwise overall sand yellow vehicle exhibited this camouflage on its barrel. **31** Also all accessories, which will later be placed on the model, will receive their basic paint by airbrush.

Step by Step -- In the following stages, I would like to describe the weathering of the model step-by-step, by using different components of the subject as examples.

FILTER - 32 The first filter applied over the entire model is very important. It satisfies two roles; firstly to act as an ordinary filter and, secondly, to break the surface tension of the model. Therefore, this first filter must be mixed with a drop of dish-washing liquid, so that the water- diluted acrylic paint is not repelled from the model's surface, but merges with it. Only with this first filter do we need a drip of detergent…all subsequent layers can be diluted with ordinary water. **33** With the example of the casemate's roof, it becomes clear that I worked with other filters here. Depending on whether the component to be worked is vertical or horizontal, it will be processed in accordance with lighter or darker filters. Likewise, one can emphasise different details with slightly altered colour variations.

CHIPPINGS & RUST The paint chips have been applied in several steps. Depending on how deep the scratches have penetrated through the various paint layers, three colours (dark brown, primer red and sandy yellow) are used for further detailing. For this, the colours will be slightly brightened, to stand out from the rest of the paint, which again is positive for the depth of the model and adds more life. One should not overdo it, but it is necessary to emphasise the paint here and there, as the following weathering will cover parts of it again. The colours used for this purpose are exclusively acrylics from Vallejo. I always place a drop of paint on a pallet and mix it with some water until it attains the right consistency. With the rust, I have used this very sparingly on this model; some streaks on the armour skirts and roof structure (and on a few other selected places) are sufficient for a 'deployable' vehicle. I've used three different rust shades from Lifecolor.

CHIPPING - 34-35 It is always recommended to start the paint chipping at the edges and corners of the armour plates and to spare the large areas as far as possible. **36-37** The second chipping phase now deals with deeper scratches, which again brings to the fore the red rust protection or bare metal. **38** The finished roof of the casemate. An example of rust streaks is the rusty retaining wire for the spare track links, which was used as additional armour. **39-40** Also, the Zimmerit should receive chipping. For this purpose, a light grey was used. At those places where the Zimmerit completely is missing, rust-protection red primer was applied.

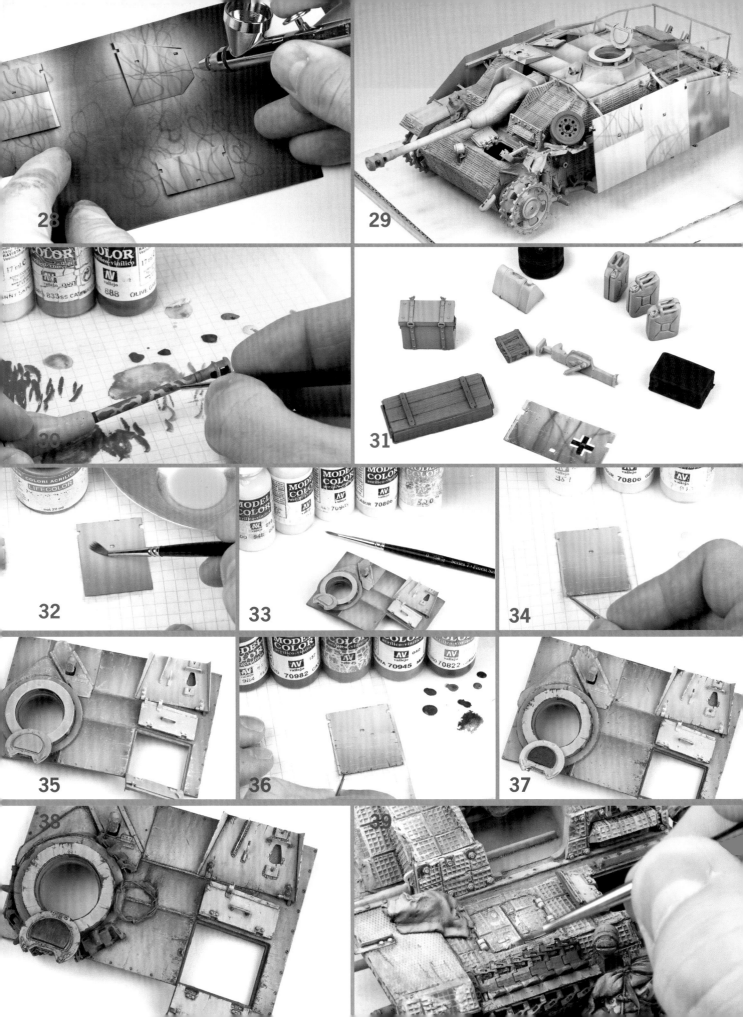

28

29

30

31

32

33

34

35

36

37

38

DEPTH OF COLOUR The most effective method of shading and, as a further strengthening of depth effect, is the classic pin-wash. All details such as joints and rivets are highlighted with a darker colour. Here, the shade is not as extensively applied as with the filter, but mainly just to screw heads, columns, and raised details. Oil colours or enamels diluted with white spirit are used normally for that task or, more recently, ready-mixed washes such as those from MIG. Here again, I only work with acrylic paints on which capillary action works in a similar manner. The degree of dilution is again crucial for the expression of capillarity. If the colour is diluted too much, it flows very quickly around all the increase but after drying, it's barely visible. However, if the colour is mixed too thickly, it will not flow around the details. Corrections and improvements are only possible as long as the paint has not dried and, thus, one should always have one more paintbrush and clean water on the workbench.

40 With a dark brown colour mix, all the details are highlighted.

SOIL & DUST APPLICATIONS Of course, contamination with soil and dust depends on where and when the vehicle was used. It obviously makes a big difference as to whether the vehicle was operated in a dry summer, or damp autumn terrain. With my StuG III, which will be presented at the end of October/beginning of November 1944, in Hungary, mud and wetness will dominate.

41 Several different brown acrylic colours were incorporated into the surface of the model, wet on wet (872 Chocolate Brown, 825 Cam. Violet Brown, 873 US Field Drab, 916 Sand Yellow, 837 Pale Sand). 42 Subsequently, mud and stronger earth contamination followed. Here is a picture of the material used for the representation of that detail. 43-45 Preparation of the surfaces which are to receive heavier contamination. 46 Mud splashes were applied with the help of an airbrush. 47 The representation of wetness represented the last step in the contamination of the lower hull and suspension. This was achieved by dabbing Tamiya X-19 Smoke on the appropriate places. I also applied leaves from PlusModel.

ACCESSORIES & DETAILS All the many small details have a huge impact on the final appearance; one should therefore pay particular attention to the representation and the painting of these components. For example the spare track links, distributed across the whole vehicle, should be provided with a variety of colours to give the viewer the impression that they have different origins. Many areas of the model can be arranged more interestingly and, with more life, by the placing of properly considered accessories.

48 A fine example to emphasise the front of the vehicle. The spare track links, as well as the fastened and lashed equipment, are beautiful eye-catchers at this point. 49 The spare wheel serves as a further variation and touch of colour. 50 A view of the mounting brackets

of the additional filters. Also with such small detail, one should proceed with very careful painting. **51-52** Vehicle markings were partly painted by hand. The vehicle identification number on the right side and black Balkenkreuz on the left side, were provided with streaks of expired paint in order to emphasise changes of some of the skirts. **53** Spare track links were primed with grey-blue Tamiya metallic. **54** Subsequently, the individual track links were painted with different colours from Vallejo. **55** Afterwards, spare track links were attached to the model and I continued with the further weathering. **56** The attachment of Plexi-glass covers in front of the periscope, on the commander's cupola.

TRACKS & WHEELS The wheels got the same treatment as the rest of the vehicle…detail-washing, paint chips and dirt. For the greasy marks, I mixed Vallejo 950 Flat Black with 984 Flat Brown, together with Tamiya

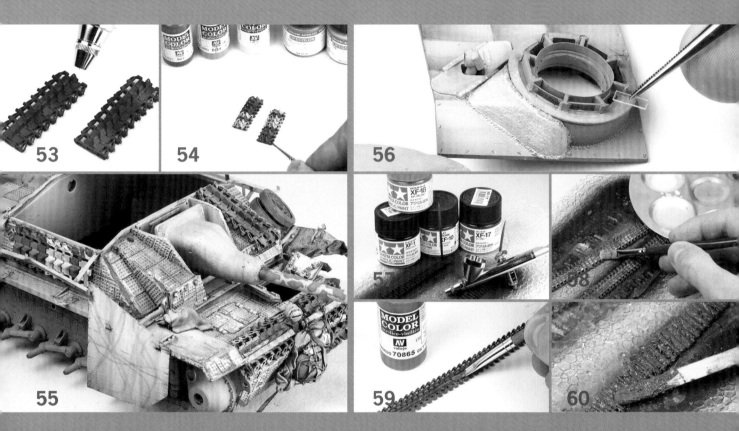

X-22 Clear. The rubber rings of the wheels received a mixture of Black and Vallejo 820 Off-White. Since the drive-sprockets and idler-wheels are subject to constant abrasion from the tracks, I painted those areas with Vallejo 865 Oily Steel and 864 Natural Steel. **57** The tracks first got a base coat of Tamiya paint by airbrush. **58** Then, they were treated with several washes of acrylic paint. **59** Those areas which come in contact with the ground or the wheels were dry-brushed with a small flat brush and Vallejo 865 Oily Steel. **60** The tracks were treated with the same mud mixture as used on the lower hull and the chassis.

with my vignette Farewell to the Faith, I of course needed several figures. After countless samples, new ideas and adjustments, it finally became 11 figures in total. Even though I have frequently regretted using this large number of subjects during the construction and painting, because it meant a lot of work, I'm very content with the overall scene and wouldn't have excluded

any of the characters. Since each figure was adapted individually to the vehicle and the scene, most figures had to be partly modified and converted with the help of different figure sets.

Since the main topic of this article is the StuG itself, though, I did not want to delve too deeply into the figures, which already represents its own topic. Therefore I would

simply like the photos of the figures to tell the story.

Mud, wetness & cold

The last part concerns the construction and design of a suitable base for the model. I do not want to deal with this topic in detail too much because this is beyond the scope of this article.

THE FINISHED MODEL By looking at the pictures of the completed StuG, it is clear what influence all the little details have on its final appearance. All the various dots of colour and weathering lead to more successful surface interaction. In the following pictures I photographed the model without its armour skirts. Here one receives an unobstructed view of the chassis and the illustrated front 'heaviness'. Even as a single model, the StuG III makes a great impression!

FAREWELL TO THE PAST

However, the task of the base should always be to support the mood and atmosphere, or in short, to supplement the whole story. Generally, I try to create three different levels, each one having the task of moving the main story and the main part of the vignette into the centre point. Obviously, the background is behind the main scene and should give the whole thing, visually, more height. The tree represents this background element in my vignette, while the addition of the river offers deeper level for overall harmony.

Each element of a diorama or a vignette should be designed with the same care and attention, because as with a chain, the complete work is only as strong as its weakest link.

The bridge

This was made entirely of Styrodur. First of all, the rough shape of the later component was cut out of the Styrodur plate. Then the structure of the brick wall was carved in to the material. After grouting of the brick wall and some paint and weathering, the whole component was fitted into the base.

The tree

There are many good methods and techniques for producing realistic trees, but the best bases almost always feature natural plant parts, such as roots and small branches. With this tree I used remainders of an appropriate plant for the trunk and the larger branches. The smaller boughs were created from sea foam. After the painting, some branches received after-market leaves from MiniNatur. These leaves are typically made of paper or thin card, and must be first painted and subsequently brought into form. Then, they were glued on piece by piece.

The groundwork

The actual base was made of styrofoam, which first was framed with plywood. Then I formed the surface with plaster, followed by a mixture of water, white glue and fine earth. I designed the vegetation

THE BRIDGE - 61-62 The structure of the brick wall was carved into the Styrodur with the help of a scalpel and individual joints were enlarged slightly with a corresponding tool. The bridge finished, ready for the base colours. **63** The base coat of the bridge was rendered with acrylic paints from Tamiya. **64** The brick structure was then grouted with ordinary plaster. **65** The finished bridge intended for installation into the base.

THE TREE - 66 The tree in its raw state; the tree trunk was revised with Magic Sculpt and received a bark structure. **67** The painted tree....eventually, leaves were attached, along with a little moss in random areas. **68** After the tree was attached to the base, the roots were modelled using Magic Sculpt.

with the help of various products from the MiniNatur range, as well as brush bristles for the longer grass. The ivy on the bridge also comes from a MiniNatur, but contrary to the instructions was processed leaf by leaf. For the small segment of the river, I used epoxy resin (a two-part resin product by Faller), which was poured in several thin layers, each slightly tinted. Before the final layer was completely dried out, several leaves were incorporated into the water layer. The puddles and the slush on the road were developed likewise with this casting mass, but this time with a different colouring.

After completion of all work, the plywood framework of the diorama was disguised with thin oak wood veneer, which was then coated with several layers of wood stain. The lower frame was sawn out of wood strips, while the name plate was designed on a PC, printed on foil and glued onto a tailored plastic plate.

Volker Bembennek

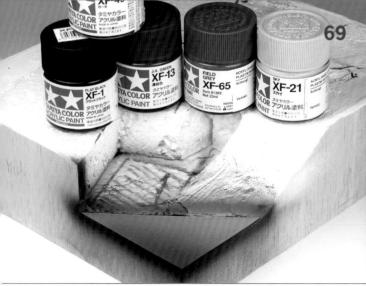

69

70

THE BASE - 69 The actual base was made of Styrofoam, which was initially dressed with a plywood frame. 70 The rear part of the vignette in the raw state; the grass was mostly created from brush bristles. Also the tree was test fitted here. 71 The epoxy resin (a two-component resin product by Faller) to represent the water surface was applied in several thin layers, each slightly tinted. 72 The almost-finished base. Note that there are cutouts for the tracks of the assault gun. This is necessary to let the vehicle later sink in the muddy terrain and give it a realistic look. The border post along the road was made of Styrodur.

72

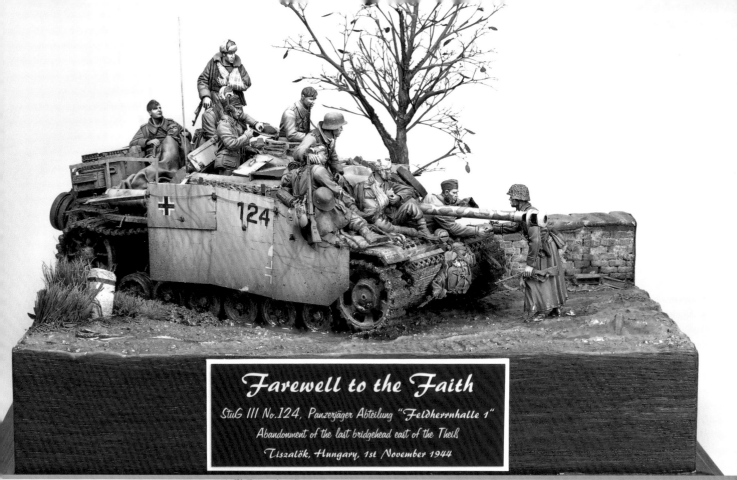

Farewell to the Faith

StuG III No.124, Panzerjäger Abteilung "Feldherrnhalle 1"

Abandonment of the last bridgehead east of the Theiß

Tiszalök, Hungary, 1st November 1944

THE LAST OF THE BREED

Text and model by **Toni Canfora**

The editor made his choice early. The series of wartime photos of a late-war StuG abando-ned in Czechoslovakia were far too attractive to resist reproducing. With help from a pile of literature, he embarked on the build of this Alkett-constructed, three-tone camouflaged warrior from Jan/Feb 1945.

While Panther and Tiger tanks are ever-popular subjects among mo-dellers and historians, they only served in relatively small numbers…and some vari-ants for a rather short period of time. The Sturmgeschütze, conversely, served throug-hout the war and was built in large numbers - and served virtually on every front that the German forces were deployed. These circumstances give modellers unlimited op-tions in terms of modelling the StuG.

It's also very interesting to see the de-sign development of the StuG, constantly upgraded and modified based on combat experience for one, but also due to shor-tages of raw materials. From its early fire support role, the StuG subsequently tur-ned into a capable tank killer and served well in defensive roles.

My model depicts one of the late ver-sions of the G model, in this case produ-ced in early 1945 at the Alkett factory. It may seem strange that a production date can be determined to within the span of a few months, but with good references and a number of conclusions many alternative options can be ruled out. In my case, I extensively used an excellent book from History Facts, covering all modifications

the StuG went through, listed piece-by-piece, date-by-date; an absolute must for anyone with a great interest in the StuG. An interesting thing that struck me while researching this model, was that where many modellers are real nit-pickers when it comes to Tigers and Panthers, many StuGs seem to be built in a more 'anyth-ing goes' fashion. I personally think that this back-bone combatant deserves better and more accurate treatment.

Which to build?

There have been many kits of the StuG over the years, and most variants are now available or can be achieved with some modification using aftermarket offerings, or scratch-built parts. A late version, which in my world means from October 1944 and after, was released by Dragon in the late 1990s and is not up to today's standards, even if a good model can be built from it … if you can find one, that is.

I decided to opt for Dragon/Cyber-hobby's more recent release, the StuG Ausf.G May 1944 production, as a star-ting point. This kit is highly detailed and (fairly) accurately represents what it says it is, though there are errors present. Ho-

wever, that didn't bother me too much as I was going to convert it into an early 1945 production machine anyway. Apart from reference books I was also fortunate to have access to a number of photos of a late production StuG, photographed in Czechoslovakia after the war. These hel-ped me to identify various key details of late production StuGs.

So, how do we determine a late StuG from an earlier version? An Alkett vehicle from that produced by Miag? Well, I will not go into every single detail as the list would be long and hard to limit, but I will try to point out a few of the typical featu-res. Also, keep in mind that the StuG was modified all the way to the end of the war and smaller adjustments were made on the very last StuGs to leave the factory.

Here are some of the changes implemen-ted on the StuG from the summer of 1944:

- Cast saukopf mantlet with opening for co-axial machine gun (Alkett only, Sept -44. Miag bolted rectangular from May, -44)
- Rotating machine gun (Oct -44)
- Close defence grenade launcher (Oct -44)
- Five roof attachment points for the two-ton crane (from Oct -44)

STUG III AUSF. G

The overview of the assembled, unpainted model reveals all the various modifications to improve the detail and to date it to early 1945. The PE fenders were not glued, but soldered for better strength. Note the Alkett-style return rollers, gun travel support and tow beam, which were all taken from an old DML kit.

- Rear engine deck plate attached with four bolts (Alkett June -44, Miag May ,-44)
- Bolted towing beam on bottom rear hull (Alkett Dec -44, Miag Nov -44)
- Frontal towing eyes with stops (Alkett from Jan -45, Miag from Nov -44)
- Gun barrel travel support (Alkett from July -44, Miag June -44)
- Muzzle brake with larger circular faces (June -44)
- No hub cap on drive sprocket, small centre hole (March -44)
- Roof top secured with raised hexagonal screws (May-44)

Except for the list above there were other small changes too, so please check your references for a full coverage.

Construction

The building of the kit was rather straightforward, although checking references was necessary throughout the project, as the basic kit for Dragon's G StuGs is the early G, so pay close attention to which parts are to be used.

The only modification made to the chassis and running gear was the replacement of the return rollers. Those supplied in the kit are the usual rubber style and the steel type with spokes. I was fortunate to be able to cannibalise the correct return rollers from an old kit provided by my fellow modeller Roger Hurkmans. From this kit I also sourced the horizontal tow bar which is characteristic for the late StuGs from November 1944.

I used the kit's drive sprocket but removed the centre screw and drilled a small hole, which was used to hold the sprocket in place in the lathe at the factory. The kit included decent individual track links, but they were the wrong type for my model so employed Friulmodel items instead.

Moving on to the hull, I decided to replace the fenders with photo-etched items from Voyager and these were soldered, rather than glued. I used the kit fender supports though, as I needed the pressed metal version used by Alkett. From June 1943 Alkett used pressed metal on the first and fourth support bracket, and Miag the tubular versions. This topic seems to be one that many modellers simply ignore and they don't check references. I scratch-built the late style tow cable brackets, as well as the holder for the C-hooks and, then, added the typical German tool clasps … in this case from Aber's range.

The kit's 80mm-thick front plate seemed slightly undersized, so I decided to replicate the thickness by adding a piece of plastic card and, reinforced the weld seems using Magic Sculpt. The gun travel support was also taken from the cannibalised kit and a coil spring was added to it. On the rear plate, minor surgery was

1 In this photo we see the tow beam introduced on late StuGs. Also note the PE chains. **2** Although little of the interior is visible on the finished model, this area received proper painting and weathering attention all the same. **3** Cast serial numbers on the mantlet were re-created by carefully shaving off digits from a kit sprue, then melting them into place with liquid cement. **4** The fastening hooks for the engine hatches were made from metal sheet and copper wire.

4 The model was first given a coat of Citadel Chaos Black… **5** …then an initial coat of green. **6** This was followed by various colours to achieve the desired camouflage pattern. **7** The camouflage was then shaded and highlighted for greater depth. **8** Sponge and fine brushes were used to apply the Vallejo acrylics to simulate chipping. The washes were carried out with oils and Tamiya panel line wash.

required to represent the late-style back plate with just four bolt heads.

The engine deck was upgraded with photo-etched holders for the cleaning rods, and a Tamiya toolbox with Aber clasps was taken from my scrap supply. In fact, most brackets, clasps and tool holders were 'donated' by numerous left-overs from older German projects. To the back of the stowage railing I also added two large metal sheets, which look like a pair of schürtzen; these were prominent in my reference photos and added originality.

My reference vehicle didn't have any schürtzen, or even brackets for them. This is probably explained by the shortage of material at the assembly line by the end of the war.

The gun barrel was sourced from RB Model, while the saukopf was taken from the kit. I added the cast serial number on it and gave it some extra texture, by using diluted Tamiya putty. A hole was also drilled for the co-axial machine gun as the kit part represented the saukopf without the port.

From October 1944 the StuGs sported mounts for attaching a jib crane on the compartment roof and these were made from hollow plastic rod, cut to correct length and slightly rounded at the top. On the commander's cupola I added the plexi-glass covers and steel wire for the closing mechanism on the hatch.

The assembly of the kit would probably have been more straightforward if it wasn't for the modifications, but much time was spent on reference checking so I was very pleased when the construction was done and painting could begin.

Painting

It's always hard to determine a camouflage pattern from a black and white photo. Many factors such as lightning conditions, weathering and not least photo quality play their part. So, this means we are stuck with making conclusions based on facts from references and, a little imagination. In my case, I had reference photos to hand of the individual machine I was modelling, along with other photos of late production StuGs.

From January 1945, no German factory was longer allowed to paint the vehicles

9 The first layer of mud comprised plaster, Humbrol enamel and fine sand. 10 Various Humbrol shades were used to blend the mud colours and make certain areas look damp. 11 Accumulated dust on the fenders was also created with oil and Humbrol paints. 12-13 Fine sand, dry forest litter, paper leaves and Humbrol were mixed and applied to further simulate the vehicle's ingrained dirt. 14 Washes were also applied to the road wheels, idler and drive sprocket.

in the yellow base coat; all vehicles were to use the green base coat already implemented on Panthers and King Tigers, and the camouflage of dark yellow and brown was factory applied. When studying photos I was at first convinced that my StuG had a yellow base coat and, since it sported the rear hull plate tow bar introduced in December 1944, I made the conclusion that it was a December -44 production machine. However, the more I studied the photos, the more convinced I became that the base coat was actually green. Add

to that the fact that my vehicle still carried the air deflector below the engine outlets, which were removed in March 1945, I could quite certainly determine the vehicle to be produced between January and February 1945.

So, I was to paint my model in a green base coat (RAL 6003 Olivengrün), with patches of yellow (RAL 7028 Dunkelgelb), and brown (RAL 8017 Rotbraun). After consideration, I decided to use the Tamiya range as I'm very familiar with it and the paaint usually performs very well.

But first, I gave the model a coat of Games Workshop's Chaos Black, as I always do on models which are to have dark base colour. I mixed a number of Tamiya shades to achieve what I was looking for and applied several layers, subsequently lightened for greater depth.

When I was pleased with the green colour I moved on to the yellow, which was carefully applied with a very fine setting on my airbrush. This was also followed by a lighter mix to create variety to the surface. The same procedure was repeated

15 The tracks were painted with Tamiya Red-Brown, then given a heavy wash mix of Vallejo pigments and Humbrol paints. **16** The worn metal surfaces of the tracks were simulated by using fine abrasive paper and graphite pencil. **17** Tamiya Smoke was used to simulate oil stains. **18** The rear view shows the makeshift steel plates which, to echo wartime photos, were painted in various colours and mud-stained with a brush.

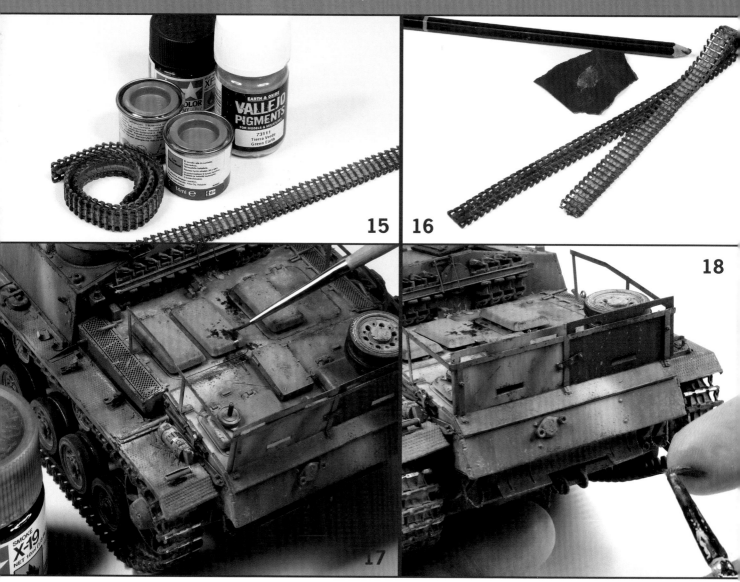

with the brown patches and finally, touch-ups were made using the green base coat. The last step was to apply a thin coat of Johnson's Klear to seal the surface for the weathering.

Weathering

Now the fun begins!...turning that plastic model into a battle-weary, realistic-looking vehicle. My first step was to apply a thin wash of diluted black-brown oils to make the colours harmonise and blend together. This was followed by a more concentrated wash, which I applied around all rivets, bolts, in weld seams and crevasses. This immediately produced greater depth and made the model look grimy. This procedure can be repeated over and over, it's simply a matter of taste how strong the contrast should be.

To simulate wear and tear, I created small chips using a sponge dipped in diluted Vallejo Acrylic colour, in this case a grey-brown mix. This process is very rewarding to perform but can be easily over-done. I have to admit that I pro-bably took it a little too far considering this vehicle's short service period, even though reference photos showed obvious damage. Keep in mind to concentrate the chipping to areas most likely exposed to climbing crew members etc. I also simulated scratches using a very fine brush and, a wider brush was used for dry- brushing the mix onto the fenders' upper surfaces.

Next was the simulation of rain marks and streaks. For this I used both oils and Humbrol enamels, which were diluted and applied in a random pattern on the

19 The plexiglass shields on the commander's cupola were cut from clear plastic sheet. **20** The late style commander's hatch had no 45° stop… instead it laid flat at 90° when open. **21** The fastening hooks for the engine hatches is a feature typical of late-war StuGs. **22** The placard for the fire extinguisher comes from the Archer range. **23** Note the colour variation on the wet and dry mud.

vehicle's flat surfaces. After setting for a few minutes, a damp brush was used to create the streaks and to collect excess fluid. When creating these marks, many different colours can be used and even if they may look stark when applied, they usually blend into the surface and create an interesting colour spectrum.

To simulate mud and dirt on the chassis and running gear, I made a mix of plaster, Humbrol enamels, fine sand and a small portion of static grass. This mix was applied with a stiff brush in a random pattern.

A slightly darker and thinner mix was then applied around some of the suspension arms and randomly on the hull, to make some of the muddy areas look damp.

I'm not too fond of using pigments so, to blend the muddy colours and transfer them onto the upper hull and fenders, I again turned to Humbrols and oils. Thin

washes were applied first on the muddy areas on the chassis, then on the fenders and into the corners of the upper hull. The same mix was also used on the upper hull sides to simulate streaks. As a final touch, paper leaves and fine sand were

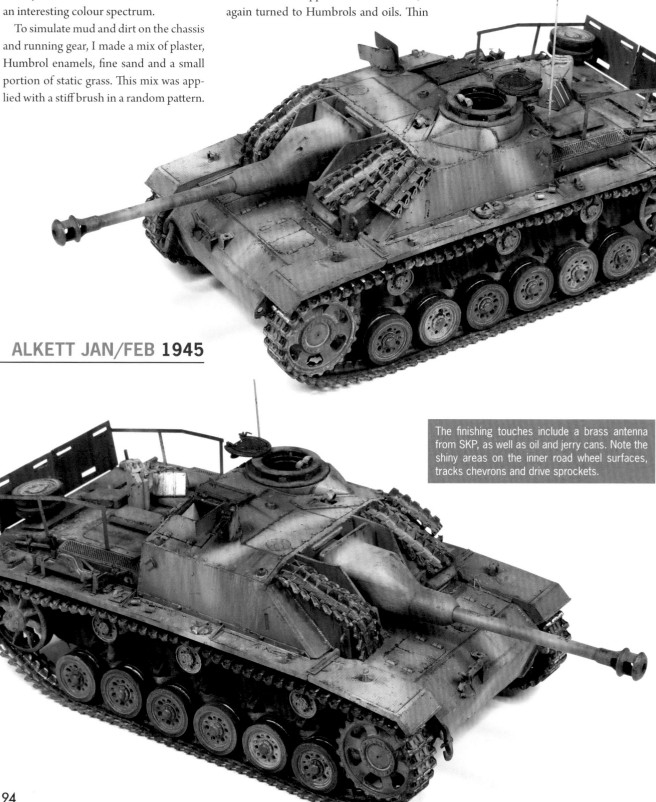

ALKETT JAN/FEB 1945

The finishing touches include a brass antenna from SKP, as well as oil and jerry cans. Note the shiny areas on the inner road wheel surfaces, tracks chevrons and drive sprockets.

blended into the mix and applied on the fenders and randomly on the engine deck, to further enhance the appearance of accumulated dirt.

The tracks were painted red-brown using Tamiya, followed by several washes of Humbrol and Vallejo pigments, mixed with a small amount of plaster. To simulate the shiny metal surfaces I used a fine grit abrasive paper to sand off the paint. The guide horns and inner surfaces were treated with a lead pencil. Road wheels and drive sprockets were also given a shine using printer's ink mixed with a small amount of black oil paint.

Finishing off

The wood and Bakelite on the tools were hand-painted using acrylics, as was the blue tail light. SKP makes the very fine antenna...an item that saves much time

in comparison to scratch-building. I also added a couple of oil and jerry cans, as well as one of the spare road wheels. To simulate mud stains I dipped a small brush in diluted Humbrol and splattered it in a random pattern, mainly on the rear hull plate. Some of the most exposed areas of the hatches and edges were carefully treated with a graphite pen to simulate wear. Oil stains on the engine deck were created by carefully adding dots of semi-translucent Tamiya Smoke, and this was also added around various bolts on the road wheels.

Conclusion

I had plans to place this model in a vignette for this book, as I think most models look best on a base, but that will have to be for the future. Although I won't feel I'm 100% finished until I do, I'm still

pleased that I followed my plan; to make an accurate, late-production Alkett StuG. However, I'm sure there are faults on my model that I'm not aware of and no matter how hard we try, there seems to be endless exceptions to the rule regarding tank production.

I would like to once again thank Peter Müller for sharing his wide knowledge of this vehicle, and Marek Solar for letting me use his fantastic wartime photos as a source of inspiration and guidance.

Toni Canfora

Although designed as an infantry assault vehicle, the StuG was very potent tank hunter due to its low profile. The finished model clearly displays the late war camouflage pattern.

THE LAST OF THE BREED

Other titles from Canfora Publishing

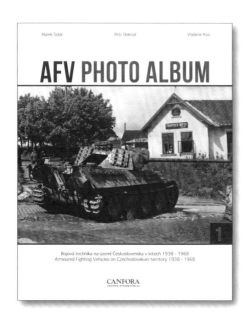

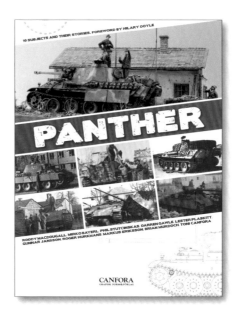

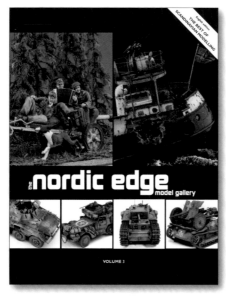

Online shop: www.canfora.se

CANFORA
GRAFISK FORM&FÖRLAG